HOW AND WHY
AMERICANS
GO OFFSHORE

HOW AND WHY

AMERICANS GO OFFSHORE

- Profit
- Privacy
- Protection

Dr. Larry Turpen

HAYNES & ASSOCIATES
PUBLISHING

CUPERTINO, CALIFORNIA

Originally published as *Offshore Options for Small Businesses*
© 1990, by Dr. Larry Turpen
Published by Intercon Associates, Ltd.

How and Why Americans Go Offshore. © 1994, by Dr. Larry Turpen
Published by Haynes & Associates, Publishing

This publication and accompanying material is designed for your personal education. References to business or tax laws are believed to be
reliable at the time this publication was written. This publication is sold
with the understanding that neither the publisher nor the author is
engaged in rendering legal, accounting, security, or other professional
advice. If legal advice, accounting advice, security investment advice,
tax advice, or other expert professional assistance is required, the services of a competent professional with expertise in the required area
should be sought.

Illustrations by Christie Beniston
MacDermid Design, San Francisco, CA

Printed in the United States of America
98 97 96 95 94   5 4 3 2 1

Library of Congress Catalog Card Number: 94-75133

ISBN 0-9639092-1-5

Dedication

To you—the reader!

Many books are dedicated to friends and family who give of
their time and attention so that the
writer can go into hibernation and write. It goes without
saying that this book is dedicated to
them.

But far more important is the notion that you the reader
have now taken a giant step in
understanding that your financial well–being is infinitely
better off when you learn to think
internationally. The first step is to get beyond your own
mental and geographic borders and
"Go Offshore."

This book is dedicated to that understanding. May your life
be better for having taken the time to
read it.?

Contents

Abbreviations

ACLU	American Civil Liberties Union
AET	Accumulated Earning Tax
AOI	Associate Offshore Institute
APT	Asset Protection Trust
CEO	Chief Executive Officer
CFC	Controlled Foreign Corporation
CIA	Central Intelligence Agency
DEA	Drug Enforcement Administration
DMV	Department of Motor Vehicles
EC	European Community
EC/EU	European Community/European Union
ECM	European Common Market
EU	European Union
FBI	Federal Bureau of Investigation
FIMBRA	Financial Intermediaries, Managers & Brokers Regulatory Association.
FLP	Family Limited Partnership
FOI	Fellow Offshore Institute
INTERFIPOL	International Financial Police
IRS	Internal Revenue Service
ITPA	International Planners Association
LAD Financial Services	Life After Dentistry
Ltd.	Limited
MOI	Master Offshore Institute
NASD	National Association of Security Dealers
NCIC	National Crime Information Center
OECD	Organization for Economic Cooperation Development
RICO	Racketeer, Influence, & Corrupt Organization
SEC	Securities and Exchange Commission
TECS	Treasury Enforcement Communication System
TRA '86	Tax Reform Act

Introduction

Over the last few years, I have had the privilege of being a featured speaker on "The Use of Small Business Corporations for Privacy, Protection, and Profits" at seminars and symposia all over the world. After each presentation many people asked if I had written a book on the subject.

Therefore, I have written this book at the request of my audiences and to address one of the most prominent notions in the United States today. The notion is that any company "offshore" is by definition suspect. This is far from true. "How and Why Americans Go Offshore" defines offshore as nothing more than somewhere else from where you are. An enormous amount of legitimate business is handled offshore by many countries.

Europeans have long since come to grips with the concept and use of offshore strategies. Past war experiences are the main reason for total acceptance on their part. Europeans know that borders can change and that diversification of assets across borders is a good strategy for lifelong security.

Americans are just now looking offshore for diversification of assets. Americans are beginning to see the advantages both in asset protection as well as privacy and profits. "How and Why Americans Go Offshore" looks at legal ways to gain access to a world beyond our borders. This book presents strategies the very rich have used for years and addresses how to take these ideas and work them into your own planning.

"How and Why Americans Go Offshore" was originally published in 1990 under the title "Offshore Options for Small Businesses." The first book began with expanding the presentation notes from seminars, which were distributed to each participant. Soon others, not in attendance, began requesting a copy of the notes. This meant writing the notes more clearly. Before I knew it the notes expanded into a book on the subject.

Now, with the passage of time and the gaining of more years of experience, I feel the subject needs further expanding and an evaluation from a more logical basis. There is a need to look at just **How** and **Why** Americans now feel the need to move a certain portion of their assets offshore to a safe haven.

Americans Go Offshore for Four Reasons

1. Business: Directed to the small-business person, it is about doing business freely without the overextended hand of government monitoring every step. All business activities have certain things in common, no matter what type of business.

2. Privacy: Doing it your way, privately, with the knowledge that your success or failure is the result of your own actions; taking the results of your success to the bank; building an international retirement account.

3. Protection: Protection of your assets and hard-earned profits in a litigious world where it seems everyone including your own government, wants to share in the wealth.

4. Profits: The profits earned in a business that crosses borders and takes advantage of laws in other jurisdictions. And how the small business is very much like big business where the rules of business operations are similar.

"How and Why Americans Go Offshore" takes a closer look at the many types of business organizations in the United States, as well as in the rest of the world. Due to the unique tax status of United States citizens foreign structures take on a special importance. This book presents the most advantageous type of structure for doing most any type of business.

A Guide to the Foreign-Based Corporation

Clearly, we live in a world that is changing. Whereas U.S. laws may be more restrictive than they were in the past, other countries have become more free in some respects. There are many ways to do the job at hand. Our plans for the future must include a world outlook. We need only look to Eastern Europe where the Russian empire is breaking up and driving hard toward a market economy.

The principles of small business corporations are the same for nearly all business activities. If a business already operates in, or buy and/or sell products and/or services from a foreign jurisdiction, there is no question that this business should consider setting up a foreign-based company or trust residing in the best possible foreign jurisdiction.

"How and Why Americans Go Offshore" discusses the importance of a world perspective of setting up and meeting offshore business activity specifications. There is a section on dealing with the invasion of privacy that is being perpetrated on the American people regardless of the assurances as outlined in the Fourth Amendment of the Constitution.

There are many reasons for concern. To those of us brought up with the notion that our Constitution provides personal safety we are confronted with a frightening picture today. The actions by the U.S. government in the area of 'confiscation of property without due process', under the rules established by RICO and the DEA are at the same time frightening and sobering. The United States is no longer the land of the free and the home of the brave.

It is incredible to me that even as I write this the United States is becoming more restrictive and more repressive, while at the same time the former Soviet Union and other former communist countries are showing signs of democracy and freedom.

While we still have the freedom to look beyond our borders for solutions -- there is hope. I am a positive person, one who looks for solutions rather than to bemoan the obstacles. This drive for solutions led me into the profession of an international financial and business consultant, and provided another reason to write this book.

"How and Why Americans Go Offshore" presents all the facts regarding incorporation and the use of the corporate structure for business or investment in a foreign land. This book presents a complete explanation of corporate structure, multicorporate interaction, and the use of corporations for financial privacy, asset protection, and unbelievable profit. Also presented is the use of a trust in the international marketplace. A trust is a very valuable tool and offers special characteristics that are not available in any other entity.

Currency Anchors and Financial Strategy

Consider world economics while preparing business and financial plans. What happens in London, Tokyo, or Bonn have a profound effect on what happens in Washington, DC or in your home town.

As the world's economic picture evolves, three world giants will become clearly dominant. The three world giants will be the United States with its affiliated countries in the Americas; Japan with the economic tigers of the South Pacific; and the European Community/European Union (EC/EU), formally known as the European Common Market (ECM), led by Germany, England, and France.

All international transactions involve considerations of currency and international exchange rates. The global business person can look forward to no more than five units of exchange that can be relied upon to anchor transactions.

The five units of exchange are: 1) U.S. dollar, 2) EC/EU anchored to the German mark, 3) Japanese yen, 4) British pound, and 5) Swiss franc. Although Great Britain will be a member of the EC/EU, the British pound sterling will still be a dominant currency due to the historic and strategic importance of London as the international banking and investment capital. The Swiss franc will continue to retain its value as the most solid and stable currency in the world.

5

Europe, an Open Window of Opportunity

The year 1992 was a significant year in the history of world economics. This was the year the EC/EU took the first formal steps to remove all national borders and become, for all practical economic purposes, one single country.

The EC/EU holds economic advantages for businesses in sales, marketing, service, investments, or finance. Some small businesses may already be dealing with one or two important clients there or may include only an investment or holding company. Yet each of these will need a foothold in Europe after 1992.

There is some talk about restricting foreign trade within the EC/EU for the first five (5) or ten (10) years after 1992 to give the members of the community a chance to adjust to each other. The present offers a critical opportunity to the small-business person. Small businesses should be getting their structure in place in Europe now, so they can effectively deal in the international market over the next ten (10) to fifteen (15) years and avoid future restrictions.

Britain–Linked Isles and Former Crown Colonies Unique Advantages

I believe that the Channel Islands, the Isle of Man, Gibraltar, the Bahamas, the British Virgin Islands, and the Cayman Islands offer unique advantageous avenues to the awakening European economic giant. These island nations, former members of the British empire, are in a very important and strategic position as offshore jurisdictions.

Though each island is now or was formally a unit of the British Commonwealth, each country has a very independent business and banking infrastructure. This infrastructure gives these small island countries an opening into the economic structure of Europe without being active members of the EC/EU.

I consider the Isle of Man or the Channel Islands as the best offshore jurisdiction for purposes of company formation and the registered home office of any expanding business or investment plans. This is because of the economic opportunities into the economic structure of Europe without being an active member of the EC/EU.

"How and Why Americans Go Offshore" includes detailed sections on the Isle of Man and the Caymans, describing the laws and services available to businesses that choose to domicile there, or in similar offshore jurisdictions throughout Europe and the Caribbean.

Intercon Associates— Experts in Foreign–Based Corporations

Intercon Associates is an Isle of Man company, with branch administrative offices in London, our function is to assist clients in establishing and managing their foreign business entity. Over the past five years, in an effort to meet client needs, our operations expanded to include Intercon Associate offices in Ireland, Gibraltar and the Cayman Islands.

Generally, the operations serve only as the functional operative of the corporate entity only. The client holds the title of managing director or managing consultant, retaining an active role in the administration of the assets and activities of the business venture.

Economists believe that after 1992 Europe will take over the position of world economic leader occupied by the

United States after the war through the 1960s and 1970s, and assumed by Japan in the 1980s. People who have prepared for this event will be in a position to make buckets of money. Intercon Associates is in the business of making the "bucket," so that when the opportunity presents itself people will have a proper and safe place to put the money.

After reading "How and Why Americans Go Offshore" you will be better informed about the rules and regulations of international business activity and ready to take advantage of this golden opportunity. It is not difficult to look beyond our borders and to establish a profitable extension of a business offshore. Intercon Associates is available to help you in any way we can.

To that end, Intercon Associates wants to stress that our purpose is to create and manage the corporate entity, leaving the client free to build and manage the business activity and wealth. As active members of several international tax planning associations we strive to always assure our clients that the entity created for their use are both legal and safe.

All of the forms necessary to establish your business structure, to set up your foreign accounts, and a schedule of fees for this service are available upon request. Information is provided in the back of "How and Why Americans Go Offshore" to order forms. Or write to the United States. representative office in Reno, Nevada, or to the administrative office in London.

Best wishes as you expand your horizons to the rest of the world.

Dr. Larry Turpen
for Intercon Associates, Ltd.
Isle of Man & London

1
Global Strategies

The Year 2000—A Different World

The world of business is changing along with the rest of the world. Electronic communication and low-cost travel have made it much smaller. In addition, no longer is the United States of America the most prominent country politically and economically. Though, with the collapse of communism in the former Soviet Union we are unquestionably the worlds only military super-power.

After World War II, the United States set up reconstruction plans for both Japan and Europe. Japan and Europe have made the best of U.S. assistance and in many ways they are looked upon as equals in the world scene. The United States now shares the economic power with the other giants of the world.

U.S. citizens are now beginning to see the impact of a world community, a global village where all people are economically dependent on each other. Countries, once contained by the Iron Curtain, now access many international market strategies and are fast becoming more similar to democratic countries.

Though hard times are a reality today, the Japanese have the 10 largest banks in the world and an effective monetary strangle-hold on the world's economy. Japan sells, lends, and saves, while the U.S. buys, borrows and spends. In late 1988, the Japanese had personal savings of over $4 trillion, and Japanese companies had surplus liquid cash of over $1.5 trillion looking for international investments.

The European Economic Community

In 1992, Europe became a very different place as the European Community/European Union (EC/EU) formally came into being. The establishment of this economic giant serves to unify a population of 350 million with a standard of living similar to that of the United States. The EC/EU population has the will to change the way they live.

England, Germany, and France are leading the way to bringing economic consolidation to the European people. The EC/EU will materially affect the way Americans live and change the United States standing in the world.

People within the EC/EU are now able to move and work in other European countries without passports or visas. Eventually the EC/EU plan calls for one dominant European currency, one set of manufacturing standards and one giant market. The EC/EU will be able to move products between countries with no duty or delay.

The United States Economy

The United States of America is looking at some very hard times after the turn of the century for at least six significant reasons.

Target Years 2000 - 2020

. The Baby Boomers

. The Baby Bust

. Life Expectancy

. The Deficit

. Savings and Loan

. Social Security

---

1. The "Baby Boom" generation will be coming into their retirement years, making extreme demands on the Social Security system.

2. The "Baby Bust" generation follows immediately behind, with an extreme drop in the birth rate from the previous generation. The mothers in the years following the baby boom gave birth to far less children. These children are now growing into their adulthood. Their Social Security taxes will have to increase significantly to produce the income necessary to sustain the Social Security system for the retirement needs of the "Baby Boom" generation.

3. Medical science has made it possible for all of us to live longer, requiring the need for retirement benefits longer into the future. The down side of this situation is that the number of workers required to produce the funds in the Social Security system is less and our needs will be greater.

4. Our government continues to borrow into the future to meet current needs. Congress has refused to face the demands of responsible citizens such as members of the Grace Commission, Ross Perot and others demanding that government spending be cut.

5. In spite of the extra demands by the Savings and Loan situation, insurance and banking requirements the government continues to spend.

6. Government borrows the money in the Social Security trust fund and transfers the funds into the U.S. General Treasury. The interest on the national debt is rapidly reaching a point where it can no longer be sustained.

Americans Look Offshore

The United States economy has lead many Americans to look seriously at the safety and security of their assets. It has led them to look beyond the borders of the United States to find some answers to their perplexing problems.

Only a few U.S. citizens are aware of the advantages of international diversification. For many years these citizens have used the international jurisdictional differences in the laws to build individual or business structures that have proved to be highly beneficial.

Some citizens concentrated their activities to avoid taxes or, in some cases, to engage in outright tax evasion.

Tax avoidance or tax evasion is neither wise nor necessary. Tax evasion is illegal. Structuring a business to take advantage of tax laws is legal and is the essence of good business. The use of internationally based business entities are common in the Fortune 500 companies. The law that allows Fortune 500 companies to operate in this manner is also available to the small business. Business law throughout the world offers the opportunity and the structure to legally establish yourself as a multinational operation to the laws of a particular jurisdiction.

Any small-business in the United States will be missing a big market at a turning point in history if they do not establish a strategic position now in relation to the EC/EU. This means setting up and using a foreign-based operation.

We are All in "Business"

As you read this book, you will see that it is directed to "business." I've been asked if this applies to individuals as well. I feel it is necessary to clarify this concept. Each of us, no matter what we do, is in the "business" of making money. That is, whatever we do is designed to make a profit, to better our lives, and to add to our wealth. So in this sense we are all in "business."

Tax Avoidance and Tax Evasion— How are They Different?

There are many U.S. Court decisions and statements by Supreme Court justices that affirm the right of an individual to structure their life so as to reduce and in some cases completely eliminate the need to pay taxes.

13

Judge Learned Hand, in the case of Gregory vs. Helvering, said, "Anyone may arrange his affairs so that his taxes shall be as low as possible...nobody owes a public duty to pay more than the law demands. Taxes are an enforceable extraction...and not a voluntary contribution." In explaining the difference between tax avoidance and tax evasion Justice Louis Brandeis told this story:

> I live in Alexandria, Virginia. Near the Supreme Court building is a toll bridge across the Potomac. When in a rush, I pay the dollar toll and get home early. However, I usually drive outside the downtown section of the city and cross the Potomac on a free bridge. If I went over the toll bridge and through the barrier without paying the toll, I would be guilty of tax evasion. If, however, I drive the extra mile and drive outside the city of Washington to the free bridge, I am using a legitimate, logical and suitable method of tax avoidance and am performing a useful social service by doing so. For my tax evasion, I should be punished. For my tax avoidance, I should be commended. The tragedy of life today is that so few people know that the free bridge even exists.

The objective of any consideration of offshore planning is not to "beat the government out of legitimate taxes," as so many people think. It is to structure your business life, in any jurisdiction, so as not to owe taxes. That is, we want to take advantage of the various states and country laws that are on the books around the world. We do this to give our operations a measurable advantage over our competitors. This applies to any business, including investment of funds for an international company in the international market.

It is our hope that each reader will learn about the many legitimate and proper bridges that exist, structure their lives to reduce exposure to taxation, while carrying on a proper and legitimate business operation. There is considerable interest in offshore structures by people in the United States and in most countries that rely on personal or business taxes to support the never-ending list of what the politicians call social programs for the less fortunate. These are nothing more than elaborate schemes to move money from the "haves" to the "have-nots." It is no wonder that throughout the years people with means have eagerly looked to innovative ways to protect their assets and preserve their wealth.

Business and Personal Privacy

As an individual living in a free country, I have always been concerned with privacy in both my personal and business affairs. Very little is private in America today. An individual, so inclined must learn to keep things to himself, and to disclose information reluctantly and only in response to a direct inquiry.

This is especially true in dealing with the government. Laws protect the privacy of your personal affairs. Individuals are under no obligation to divulge information to anyone, including an Internal Revenue Service (IRS) agent in an audit, except in direct answer to a direct question.

Anytime, we as Americans, involve ourselves in activities outside the borders of the U.S., we open up the possibility of an audit by the IRS. If you choose to live in a gray area, as far as the tax laws go, it is in your best interest not to openly talk about it or to be extra-forthcoming with answers. Let the inquisitor ask, simply answer "Yes" or "No."

15

LaVera Tours, Inc., and How it Grew

There are many business ventures that lend themselves perfectly to international diversification. One of these is the travel business. This is especially true of the agency or tour company that does a significant amount of international business.

LaVera Tours, Inc., began its experience in international affairs in 1975 with a program to visit Europe and take advantage of the current tax deductions available. Thus we formed LaVera Tours, Ltd.—a European continuing education tour company. LaVera Tours designed tours for medical professionals, like myself, who are required by state law to take a certain number of bona fide continuing education classes each year. We decided to set up the classes in Europe and take the classes there.

On each tour several doctors would say to me, "Larry, I have a large check here that I would like to deposit in a foreign bank, can you help me?" To them there was something sinister or illegal about it. They were unaware that U.S. citizens, including doctors, could open "secret" accounts in Switzerland.

First we explained, in detail, the notion of secrecy through numbered accounts. Then I took them to Zurich, Switzerland and introduced them to a private banker. I showed them how to open and operate a foreign bank account. Under the current law in Switzerland the ultimate beneficial owner of any account in a Swiss bank is known to some bank officer. Though the numbered accounts still exist, the notion of complete secrecy is no longer valid.

In time LaVera Tours, Ltd. outgrew its original purpose. There was more interest in the notion of international investing. As our list of clients grew, it became obvious to me there was a need for someone to help other people in setting up and operating a proper and legal foreign investment base.

In 1987 I sold my dental practice, renamed LaVera Tours to LAD Financial Services, Ltd. (LAD means Life After Dentistry), to become a full-time financial consultant with special interest and expertise in international structures, international investments, and international tax planning.

Terrifying Tales at Tax Time

Each year between January 1 and April 15 Americans are treated to a series of interesting stories, planted by the IRS, that include some "big name" tax fraud. The IRS does this to put into the American people a certain degree of fear.

The year 1989 featured Leona Helmsley who, though she paid over $30 million dollars in federal tax, was tried and convicted for not properly listing and paying an additional $1 million. Leona Helmsley,

ultimately sentenced to 4 years in prison and $7
million in fines, as an example of how tough the IRS
can be if it wants to press the issue.

The U.S. tax system is based on voluntary disclosure of
all income and on the taxpayer's ability to determine his tax
liability from the tables prepared by the IRS. The IRS can
perceive us be cheating and without the fear of possible
consequences the IRS knows that compliance will suffer,
hence the stories.

We also see a number of stories reporting that the top
500 corporations pay little or no tax. These stories are
designed to raise our consciousness and ire with regard to
"big business." The IRS sees business as the most ripe plum
for the picking. This can only be done if popular opinion
holds it in a certain degree of disrepute.

President Bill Clinton was elected in part because of the
notion that he was going to reduce the deficit by increasing
taxes on the wealthy and on the foreign companies who "are
not paying their fair share."

Early in my career I used to read these stories and
wonder how they did it. Laws are for all corporations, not
just the giant top 500. Surely they would not knowingly
break the law, and yet they were getting off with paying less
tax. I did not hold any animosity for the business
community. Indeed, I held them in a certain degree of awe
and respect.

Recently, an airline in-house magazine published a
story about how Boeing's International Aircraft Company
works. They literally have a sales meeting in the air. In a 747
in international air space 250 miles off the coast of
Washington, they consummate the sale, electronically
transfer the funds, and turn over the aircraft to their foreign

buyers. Conducting the transaction in this location saves Boeing about $10 million dollars in taxes on each sale.

Saving taxes must not be the primary reason for consideration of offshore structuring. Clearly, the best reason is for diversification and the safety this gives to your overall business and investment plans. If a side effect of this diversification includes a substantial saving in taxes, then the added benefits are many folds.

Once there was a company residing in a jurisdiction subject to state corporate tax and state personal income tax...

2
International Options

International Options for U.S. Citizens

International options for U.S. citizens begin with comprehension of the idea of international or global business diversification and investing. These citizens structure their business activities to conform to international law and then operate the business to make a profit. They then look for ways to invest the corporate profits as to create additional income for the business entity. Those individuals who complete these steps are on their way to diversify their investment holdings internationally.

It is important to look at what internationally held investment activities are legal for the U.S. citizen. After these are firmly in mind, we can see how a business structure that compounds these activities affords phenomenal opportunities. The astute U.S. citizen quite often selects global funds structured to meet the Securities and Exchange Commission (SEC) regulations. U.S. citizens directly purchase global funds through investment advisors or stock brokers. We highly recommended that our clients diversify their holdings to include at least 20% in foreign stocks or bond funds.

Among the stock funds recommended are Templeton Funds, which has a long track record of successful management of international funds. The severity of the stock crash of 1987 generally affected domestic funds far more than it did the international funds. This is one effect of diversification. That is why we make such a strong recommendation to our domestic clients.

Just as businesses are intimidated by the IRS, U.S. citizens also fear they cannot invest beyond our borders because of concerns with the IRS. There are many legitimate ways an individual can extend investment options beyond the border that are legal and profitable. Investing beyond the U.S. border provides us with a new degree of privacy, protection and excitement that previously were thought to be outside our reach.

The M&G Recovery Fund, a British-managed mutual fund, has had a phenomenal record over the last 20 years, with an average annual growth of 60%. Yet, we as Americans have not had this investment option. By law, the M&G Recovery Fund cannot be promoted in the United States or solicited by investors because the M&G Recovery Fund has chosen not to comply with the Securities and Exchange Commission requirements. There are ways to gain access to such opportunities. The IRS and the Securities and Exchange Commission rules and regulations keep U.S. citizens in the dark. Our freedom to learn and take advantage of this information is the key to success. "How and Why Americans Go Offshore" presents some of the best possible ways to invest beyond the U.S. border.

The advantages range from direct investment in foreign mutual funds to the common use of foreign bank accounts. They can include "no-bounce" checking using site drafts or buying a Class B bank and using it as a proper vehicle for investment. The freedom and knowledge to learn the operation of corporations, trusts, and captive insurance companies are available to everyone.

Every entity requires a bank account to validate its existence and provide a conduit for operations. Whatever you choose to do internationally will involve the use of a foreign bank account. A foreign bank account can be a personal account, but is probably a "business" account. This is the essential first step to internationalize your thinking.

Using a Foreign Bank Account to Gain Access

If you were to become involved internationally without the use of a foreign company or trust structure, you would simply open and use a personal foreign bank account. Using a personal foreign bank account is a lot like using a bank account in this country. In most foreign countries a personal bank account is called a "current account." A current account can be a saving account or a checking account with a checkbook, if you want one. You would generally not use the foreign bank account for small transactions primarily because local merchants will question a check drawn on an international account. There is also an expense assessment with each banking transaction.

Foreign bank account deposits are usually made by mail. Making deposits by mail is the same as mailing a deposit to a local bank (i.e., Bank of America). Simply properly endorse a first party personal or company check and send it directly to the foreign banker. There is a time delay to allow the check to go through the system. When the check is clear, you can draw on the deposits as you wish.

Foreign bankers do more than just store your money. The depositor or the designated person responsible for a business account can include a letter of instructions specifying what to do with the deposit or any other funds on deposit in that bank. We quite often ask our banker to transfer the entire balance of our company account into a different currency.

Transferring money into a different currency is usually done when the dollar is weakening against the yen, the mark or the pound. This opens the door to currency plays with our own money in our own bank. The currency plays exchange has earned as much as 27% per year on moneys in this manner alone, to say nothing of the interest earned on the account as well. There is nothing illegal about holding money on deposit outside the United States. However, the Treasury Department does require a filed form if the personal account is over $10,000 at any time in the year.

A foreign bank account is very simple to open and use. It is generally held for larger purchases or foreign investments. We generally choose to maximize the interest income by placing the money in a "high yield" checking account. This is an essential first step toward international diversification.

It is noteworthy to mention at this point that banks, insurance companies, and other business entities are quite often structured as corporations with special business licenses. In Chapter 5 "Corporate Structure" we discuss corporations in more detail. Just remember to use a corporate format for almost any business entity that is set up as a separate entity with limited liability.

International Bank Accounts Offer Unaccustomed Privacy and Security

The U.S. financial crisis and lack of security are real. The Federal Reserve Board's ability to manipulate the effects of inflation are well documented. Banks are overextended to South American countries, who will probably be unable to repay their debt. The current Savings and Loan crisis will ultimately cost the taxpayers' hundreds of billions of dollars. The estimate in summer of 1992 was over $750 billion. At the beginning of the crisis, in the first three months of 1989, there was a net outflow of over $18 billion from the Savings and Loan industry. The net loss to the Savings and Loan industry was $3.5 billion. This is a sickness that someday must be treated, no matter how hard the medicine. It is time to diversify for your own safety. It makes logical sense. More Americans are learning that the rest of the world may offer safer alternatives. The old idea of "not putting all your eggs into one basket" has never been more true.

The ideas with regard to international taxation and of government fees on bank accounts, as expressed by some of the associates around President Bush, in the early stages of the Savings and Loan crisis, tend to encourage flight capital. As this becomes more obvious many governments, including the United States, will move to prevent the exportation of capital.

Now is the time to get a nest egg of capital safely off-shore in a world-class bank that has centuries of safe banking history. The primary reason for a foreign bank account is *asset diversification*. Place some of your assets into the international market before it is outlawed. An international bank account offers privacy such as we Americans have never seen. It offers the security of well-established solid banks to choose from. Foreign governments do not require banks to lend a certain portion of their assets to banana republics, with little chance for return.

As a matter of long-standing policy, foreign banks treat accounts as a private matter. It is no one's business but yours They do not freely give information to any credit company or government agency that requests information. Both busi-

25

ness and personal accounts are a private affair. In many jurisdictions it is against the law for bank officers or employees to disclose information about the bank's customers or their accounts. Finally, foreign banks do not have to meet the stringent requirements of the Federal Reserve banking system. Therefore, funds are available for more profitable investments by the banking establishment. This equates to better returns and higher interest rates on deposits, along with more responsible bank management.

Privacy and Asset Protection

Another reason for foreign bank accounts and foreign structure is to provide asset protection. There was a day, not long ago when medical professionals worried only about the level of care they could give their patients. In today's litigation-conscious society, those days are over.

It is a fact, that in Japan the ratio of graduating lawyers to graduating engineers is 1:8. That is one lawyer to eight engineers. In the United States, exactly the opposite is true. The ratio of graduating lawyers to graduating engineers is 8:1. That is eight lawyers to one engineer. That is a lot of lawyers, let loose on the American people looking for work. Which means that you or I can very easily become victims of a lawsuit. Today, doctors must first practice defensive medicine with all of its inherent costs and then direct a major portion of their intellectual resources toward protecting the assets they have accumulated over time.

Insurance coverage for some medical specialties is virtually beyond reach. Many doctors are choosing to conceal their assets and reduce the coverage. They are aware that in the likely event of a large award they will be wiped out financially and be forced to begin again to accumulate

26

retirement assets. Plaintiff's attorneys are getting better at the task of determining the total assets held in the doctor's name and are becoming very adept at liquidating those assets to pay for judgments that are awarded in excess of the insurance coverage.

Community property laws have made it virtually impossible to transfer assets into the name of a spouse, in hope to provide a protective shield. To say nothing of the devastating effect a deteriorating marriage would have on the security of that arrangement. Attorneys have found ways to negate that defense. Funds and assets held in retirement plans such as Keogh and corporate pension plans used to be safe from the execution of judgment liens, but recent decisions have penetrated that shield as well.

Consequently, there has been a recent renewed interest in offshore asset protection. This provides a mean of getting assets beyond the reach of any creditor, including the adversarial purview of the plaintiff's attorney, the investigative eyes of TRW or the local credit bureau. There are many ways to use offshore facilities to protect assets. The common U.S. citizen does not understand much of this information. It is especially foreign to the mind of a doctor, whose entire education is enmeshed in the science of his or her profession and the art of patient care.

There are several programs that are becoming more common in building a financial fortress that extends offshore. Some of these include the foreign asset protection trust and the foreign offshore corporation. Alternatives to accumulate offshore assets, through captive insurance, are discussed in detail in Chapter 13 "Captive Insurance."

The thrust of "How and Why Americans Go Offshore" is to help the reader see himself as a business person and to assist the U.S. small business to extend its options beyond the borders of the United States. By extending options into any selected foreign jurisdiction, the creation of a shield of privacy and asset protection are guaranteed with the territory. It is an incidental benefit that is the result of the respect for privacy that other parts of the civilized world provide to business.

3
International Banking

An International Bank as Your Operational Base

Opening up a personal or individual foreign bank account is an essential first step to setting up an operational base. As stated earlier, it is legal to open and use a personal foreign bank account.

- First: Select an international clearing bank in which you have instant confidence, one of the triple A-rated banks in the international banking establishment.

  An international financial consultant can provide this information.

- Second: When offshore operations are more familiar, put your investment nest egg into an international Class-A bank, a private bank, or an international trust company with banking arrangements.

  You might also look to that account to pay for any future created structures or businesses. This will provide your future tax and business planning a shield of privacy. Services paid from a domestic bank account do not offer this shield of privacy. There are a variety of banks to choose from, such as The Royal Trust Bank of Canada that have independent banking affiliates in many of the business havens of the world. Other options are to select one of the many large Class-A banks in the orient or perhaps one of the private banks in Switzerland as a choice for your offshore custodian of funds.

There are reports that the IRS threatens banks or financial institutions with forcing the loss of their "U.S. domestic" license if they do not supply information on accounts in foreign branches. If you are concerned with the possibility of overt pressure being applied to the general offices of a trust company such as Royal Trust then we would recommend that you select a private bank like Foreign Commerce Bank in Zurich.

• Third: After a little bit of experience and careful evaluation, consider the use of a Class-B bank (brass-plate) operated by someone else in the banking business, if one should become available to you.

Some Class-B banks are good, but many are a financial sham. LAD Financial Services is generally aware of one or two Class-B banks that will protect your assets and earn the interest promised in the international marketplace. You must be able to ascertain the risks involved.

• Only as a final step, would you need to consider buying and operating a brass-plate bank for yourself. You hear quite a lot about owning and operating such a bank.

In our opinion, this should only be considered if you actually plan to accept deposits and make loans. That is, you plan to be a banker and accept the fiduciary responsibility that goes with the title. Some business advisors hold seminars on the advantages of using a Class-B bank as an investment vehicle. There is no question that there are definite advantages that go with the banking license. However, there is also another level of American federal agency watchdogs watching over every act of your bank. If you make one error and they find out, the consequences can be very severe.

Remember, a bank is a corporation, a special kind of corporation. You should decide the type of corporate entity needed to accomplish specific financial or business goals. Most of all you need to do to meet those goals, with the same degree of privacy, can be accomplished during the course of an ordinary business day of a general business corporation. This is especially true if the design of the corporate entity is of an international business or financial consultant. An international business consultant can provide you the details for using an offshore operating company with **its** business accounts to accomplish a specific business objective.

Private Banking in the Civilized World

In most of the civilized world your banker is your personal investment and business intermediary. The banker makes things happen according to your wishes. Setting up private banking arrangements is one of the most important functions of LAD Financial Services, through its affiliation with Intercon Associates, Ltd. A private banker does not meet you at the teller's window and just agree to store your money. He or she sits across the table with you in a private room and through personal consultation assists you in reaching your financial objectives.

The European Tradition of Confidentiality

There is much said about the European tradition of bank privacy. It is a way of life regardless of the status of secrecy laws. Most countries simply will not disclose information about their depositors. There is a reason for this. Europeans are more cautious because they have experienced war. They know that any day they could be living under a different government. Europeans know the borders of their country can change. It is common for Europeans to bank in a neighboring country or even in an offshore island like the Isle of Man, the Channel Islands, or Malta.

The Switzerland secrecy laws are known around the world. So is Austria and, lately, Luxembourg. The laws in these countries are designed to ensure that citizens of the world can do business in a private manner. These citizens can accumulate wealth without fear of governments or process servers making off with a portion of the profits. However, recent actions and proposed changes in the law have diminished the Swiss position in the privacy world. It is still one of the best but bears watching carefully.

Switzerland feels it must maintain its place as a responsible nation in the world community. To allow the secrecy of accounts allegedly stolen from their countries' treasuries by Ferdinand Marcos, late president of the Philippines, and Haiti's Duvaliers, undermines that international respect.

Austria, Luxembourg and many of the Caribbean jurisdictions are also still secret. Jail terms are mandatory for disclosure of information about account holders. These countries are rapidly replacing Switzerland as the most desirable place to hold private accounts. Incidentally, the Swiss say with a smile that Liechtenstein is where they keep their secret accounts. This has something to say for secrecy in this small country where disclosure is against the law, with mandatory jail sentences for lawbreakers.

Access to business records and safe deposit boxes in most countries is restricted and secret. Foreign business records are safely stored in your foreign administration office, outside the investigative eyes of U.S. government, upon request.

How to Operate a Personal Foreign Bank Account

One way you can set up a personal foreign bank account is to declare funds on deposit, in excess of the $10,000 threshold to the U.S. government. To do this, you would simply set up the foreign account and use it as an account at a local bank. You must declare the interest received as income. However, there are no 1099 Form sent to the government to confirm that interest earned. The government relies on the honor system.

If it is your intent to have a personal foreign account that is not declared to the U.S. government the account must not exceed a maximum of $10,000 at any time. This method involves a little creativity, as well as taking advantage of investments that do not accumulate declared interest or earnings. The two most prominent examples are umbrella mutual funds and hard assets. You can arrange for the bank to pay certain large bills or make large transfers for investments. You can use your balance sheet to arrange a personal line of credit on the account. Your overdraft payoff is a short-term loan that does not take the account over the limit.

It is important to reinvest profitable investment funds directly deposited into the account to protect the maximum $10,000 threshold. Buy gold and umbrella mutual funds or other non-reportable assets to keep the balance of the account below the report threshold.

Another option is to apply for a bank issued Gold American Express Card or the European Access Card, which is the European answer to the Master Card. Major banks issue these cards to qualified account holders. This is a debit card and will require a compensating deposit in the company account. However, there is no electronic connection to United States. If requested, the banker will make the payment out of the appropriate account for you. The credit card company destroys the purchase records after 90 to 120 days. These cards are good anywhere in the world. Remember... "Don't leave home without it" and "Membership has its privileges."

It is important to remember that foreign banks do more than store money. They buy securities, gold, insurance, hold your valuables in safe deposit boxes, act as your personal financial intermediary and they are just a phone call away: 011-country code-area code-number. If you feel it is necessary to have a personal account, in addition to the business account, always be aware of the dollar per currency value and keep the balance of the personal account below the $10,000 threshold.

The Use of Class–B Banks for Investment

There are several companies in the United States that approach U.S. citizens with the idea of using a Class-B or brass-plate bank as a mean of setting up and operating an investment program. There is a place in the business arsenal for brass-plate banks.

As stated earlier, if a person wants to become an inter national banker and take fiduciary control of other people's deposit money, a bank is a very good way to do the job and at the same time limit the operator's liability. There are many businesses in the United States who established and run Class-B banks for internal operations very well. However, it is rare that an individual can set up such a bank and operate it in a way that the other depositors benefit materially.

Remember that your confidence in a bank's operation rests with the individual who controls the assets of the bank. The bank's ability to offer and pay high rates of return to depositors are based on the manager's skill in finding less risky, yet high-yielding investments for the bank's funds. Not, in the fact that it is simply an offshore bank that operates outside U.S. banking regulations.

A banker must first be a good business person. He or she must convince a group of people that the bank's invest-ments will pay off. If you are unsuccessful, you will never be able to attract bona fide depositors who will stay through good times and bad. Additionally, I would not place my money into a Class-B bank that is operated by one individual. I would want the Class-B bank to be operated by a fully disclosed board of directors made up of responsible individuals who are held accountable for their actions.

35

There is no secret to offshore administration of a Class-B bank. The banker must find and continually reinvest depositors' money in investments that yield at least more than the bank pays the depositors, or both the banker and the bank are in deep trouble. Banks and insurance companies are corporations with special licenses or charters that allow them to operate in a special way. If investing corporate funds is your objective, then an international investment advisory corporation may just be the right entity for you to try.

4
Corporations

The Power and Pitfalls of Small Corporations

I have noted two major pitfalls of small corporations during my 25 years practicing dentistry under the aegis of a professional corporation and during my 15 years involved in international corporate structuring domestic as well as foreign small business corporations.

1. In most cases, the organizer or stockholder of the corporate entity does not know the power of the entity with which he or she is involved or directs and does not use it to maximum personal benefit.

   Through the years, many of my professional colleagues had "incorporated themselves" only to gain access to the pension and profit-sharing provisions of the tax law. That was all. They really did not know how to use the corporation for general business purposes.

2. Complete lack of or sloppy record-keeping. This is generally the rule with the small business or closely held one-person corporation. A small business corporation is as any other corporation where complete and accurate minutes must always be maintained. This is your first line of defense in any government audit.

   It is with the intention of addressing these two primary problems that I have chosen to go back to basic training and attempt to help people really understand simple corporate operations.

A Corporation is an Artificial Person

Much like the "trust" structure, a corporation is an artificial person that can do just about anything that a real person can do, except that it can't think. So, at the first meeting of the founders they appoint a board of directors. The board of directors have the responsibility of thinking for the corporation. The board elects officers to carry on the objectives of the corporation.

The units of ownership in a corporation are the shares of stock. Shares of stock are referred to as "stocks" in the United States. In other parts of the world they called "shares." A corporation in England, for instance, is called a Company Limited by Shares or Ltd. We see the letters Ltd., at the end of the company name, indicating a corporation.

The unique thing about a corporation is that the shareholders are limited in liability only to the amount they have invested in the shares. Additionally, the corporation is subject to the rules or laws of the established jurisdiction. Laws governing actions by the corporate board of directors are specific to the area of incorporation. Every state or country has its own laws. Corporations established in a given jurisdiction are subject only to those laws. So, before going on it is good to look closely at the rules of jurisdiction the corporation resides. Just like individuals, companies and trusts are "given birth" or founded in a certain birthplace. This is their domicile. They may choose to operate in a different location. This would be their residence.

Understanding Domestic, Foreign, International, and Offshore

The differences between *domestic* and *foreign* are sometimes confusing. This is especially true in a federation of states like the United States. Each individual state is considered domestic for its corporations. Those in the state next door is foreign. State laws affect the formation of corporations. This is why states, for example Delaware and Nevada attract corporations more than high-tax states like California and New York. National laws affect all corporations. This of course includes the federal tax code.

For our purposes, think of foreign as outside the borders of the United States. International means outside the border of the United States. International corporations are foreign companies. Offshore is international and therefore foreign. Mexico and Canada are offshore. Though they are physically connected to the United States, they are outside the U.S. border. In the same manner, Hawaii and Alaska are onshore even though they are not physically connected to the United States, they are within the U.S. border.

Domestic means being within the a state or territory belonging to the United States and foreign means being outside a state or territory belonging to the United States. So, when we speak in terms of onshore being within the United States borders and offshore being outside our borders the shoreline has nothing to do with the discussion.

When Influence is Preferable to Ownership

The uses of foreign corporations established in jurisdictions with favorable tax laws in respect to the residency of the member of the company have been well-documented in the annals of worldwide industrial concerns for many years.

Owning stock in a corporation or just holding a position of influence (i.e., manager director or consultant) is an option that provides tax advantages. The uses of foreign corporations established in jurisdictions with favorable tax laws are used by the small-business person to maximize personal as well as corporate benefits. This practice is being recommended by international business and financial planners.

It is possible to structure companies in such a way that the U.S. citizen, or indeed the citizen from any other country, is not listed as a member or stockholder. Thus, if that person has an identifiable beneficial interest it is obscure and relatively safe from discovery and claims against it. In many cases such beneficial interest and any connection to the United States citizen or company is never put in writing or disclosed.

Once such a structure is established, the U.S. citizen is free to deposit in that company assets such as cash investments or loans. The foreign corporation uses these assets to invest and to build its worldwide business activity.

You may already have a domestic business looking at expanding into a foreign jurisdiction or you may be looking into the idea of establishing a new business in a foreign jurisdiction to take advantage of the differences in jurisdiction law. If this is the case, our program is tailor made for you.

LAD Financial Services assists new and domestic businesses explore the possibility of expansion to a foreign country. Businesses such as international real estate development, publishing, or import and export are prime candidates for foreign expansion. The type of business is limited only by a persons imagination.

Gary Scott, in his seminars on worldwide investment opportunities says, "Think of anything you would like to do, and then think of the best possible place to do it."

Your business can invest in another company or in a captive insurance company. In any case, invest in companies established in a jurisdiction that favors non-resident members and exempts them from taxation. The growing assets of your company are free from taxation until such times the dividends are paid to employees, members, or stockholders.

It is possible, indeed desirable, for the investor to apply for a position with the company as managing director or consultant. As such, he or she would be in a *powerful position of influence* where decisions made in the management of the company are routinely ratified by the board of directors. In most cases, the managing consultant is given specific responsibility with regard to the source and application of funds.

The IRS requires U.S. citizens to declare and pay the appropriate taxes from income received offshore. Decisions he or she makes in connection with management of the company that help build the company in the world market does not result in income that is personally taxable.

Doctors and others in business facing legal judgments (i.e., malpractice, liability) are finding the foreign company approach to asset protection alternatives safe, as well as an interesting activity diversification. Serving as a managing director of a foreign company offers many indirect non-taxable personal benefits that increase their quality of life.

Assets moved into a foreign offshore corporation and managed by the employee grow tax-free until the board of directors vote to pay the retained earnings to the members or employees. The U.S. citizen must not be a listed stockholder or director of the company to avoid the problems associated with the Accumulated Earnings Tax (AET)

The corporate structure is probably the most common business structure in the world today. It offers so many advantages that its place is probably assured for centuries to come.

Stockholders, Directors, and Officers

The corporation owners are the stockholders. The stockholders are indirectly involved in the activities of the corporation. The stockholders elect a board of directors that influence the management of the corporation. On the other hand, the board of directors are in the position of power over the direction or objectives of the corporation.

The board of directors meet regularly and make decisions about overall policy and ratify or modify the action of the officers. The board of directors can fire and hire officers at their own discretion. The directors of a foreign company are responsible for contracting with an administrator to manage the daily activities. The administrator is the responsible officer of the corporation.

The corporate officers are the seat of power in the day–to–day decisions and activities of the corporation. The corporate officers hire and fire employees as well as buy and sell supplies. The corporate officers make investments with the corporation assets and direct the corporation activities.

All corporate officers are ex officio members of the board of directors. They may or may not be elected directors, but in all cases they serve at the discretion of the board of directors. Most corporations have at least three corporate officers: secretary, treasurer, and president. Since the corporation as an artificial person can't think, the secretary records the corporation's thoughts in the minute book. The treasurer is responsible for the corporate finances, and the president is responsible for carrying out the will of the board of directors.

Some states and some foreign countries allow one person to hold all of the board of director and corporate officer's positions. This sets the stage for a small business or one-man multinational. It is actually possible for one person alone to incorporate their business activities in more than one country, and to do business between these artificial people.

Principal Attractions of the Small Business Corporation

The small business corporation has been and continues to be the best possible tax shelter for your ongoing income stream. Nearly everything you pay for with after-tax dollars can possibly be turned into corporate expenses, if you are always alert to the possibilities. The amount of limited liability is limited to the value of the corporate shares. This makes it possible to invest in a corporation and be assured you won't loose lose your fortune.

Pension and profit sharing plans remain key benefits in the United States. The tax laws are written to encourage small–business people to look out for the long–term well–being of their employees. They are key benefits because these plans are available to the individual corporation as well as the Fortune 500. In these days of high costs of health care, a corporation's plan for its employees is still a very valuable benefit.

Supplemental health plans are available to pay the difference between the employee insurance payment and the actual procedure cost. These plans save the employee out–of–pocket costs, generally paid with after-tax dollars. These plans are also available even if you are the only employee. This employee benefit is deductible to the business entity.

Corporations also offer the flexibility to be actively involved in your foreign activities without the need to declare this involvement. To our knowledge, there are no forms that require you to list the corporate boards on which you serve. There is no need to disclose all the activities of the corporation except as listed in the minutes. Additionally, with a foreign offshore corporation these minutes are not disclosed to anyone.

Foreign corporations for the most part are identical to the domestic variety. They have the same director arrangement with officers to administer the affairs of the corporation. Foreign corporations can hire and fire employees as they see fit.

You, as an U.S. citizen can serve as a director, officer, or consultant to the foreign corporation without reporting that activity. The IRS does require you to report any income earned anywhere in the world. So, if you are paid a salary income it must be reported and the appropriate tax paid. The business activities of the corporation, beyond the salary or dividends paid to the U.S. citizen, is private and confidential. In most jurisdictions, its disclosure to anyone is against the law.

5
Corporate Structure

Types of Domestic Business Structure

The Personal Service Corporation

> The personal service corporation is the professional corporation used by physicians, dentists, lawyers, accountants and virtually any other profession where the licensed individual can incorporate their service. It should be noted that in almost every jurisdiction in the U.S. stock in the professional or personal service corporation can only be held in the name of the licensed professional. This fact would seem to eliminate these people from the advantages of foreign incorporation.

Dual-Tracking the Professional Corporation

> Through the use of *dual tracking,* one can separate activities and incorporate certain aspects of the business as a separate corporate entity. Every doctor acting as a business person knows it is possible to lease equipment, bulk purchase supplies, factor accounts receivable, or use an employee leasing service company for personnel needs. This opportunity also exists for nearly any profession.

Such corporate strategies are also open to the common C-corporation. Clearly, any service that is not directly related to the administration of professional care can be legally purchased from an outside provider. This makes *dual tracking* possible.

The doctor or accountant will form a second corporation, a general business corporation. The general business corporation is licensed, (i.e., Health Care, Inc.) and assigned all business functions of the office operations to that corporate entity. The individual then contracts through the professional corporation. The professional corporation provides all professional care to the patients attracted to the health care center, the business corporation.

The individual accepts a minimal salary from the professional corporation for contracted services. The individual will, as required by law, retain all the liability for health care and the responsibility for the patient records. All of the individual's other personal needs may be provided by their corporate entities, thereby eliminating the need to take a larger salary. If the individual's spouse is the president of the business corporation, the combined salaries can be sufficient to cover their life-style at whatever level they chose. They will need to be aware of the vulnerability of assets in common-law states.

A doctor with this set-up has very few assets and may not need to carry the high malpractice insurance, that is so burdensome to many doctors today. Of course, if the doctor chooses this route, he or she cannot hold stock in the business corporation, since this would be a listed asset. The problem would not present itself if the spouse and children owned all the stock in the business corporation and perhaps were employees of the corporation as well.

The C-corporation

All business corporations start as C-corporations. This is the traditional "small business corporation" and the most common business entity in the world today. There are more entrepreneurs in the United States than in any country on earth. It is interesting that Europe and Asia also have a large number of independent business people. Foreign small business corporations follow the same general format.

The S-corporation

The S-corporation (formerly subchapter-S) is a unique business entity available to U.S. taxpayers that is not generally available in other countries. The board of directors may elect to become an S-corporation within 75 days of incorporation, or within 75 days of the corporate year end. There are fewer advantages to the S-corporation under the 1986 Tax Reform Act (TRA '86). However, the most important advantage is *tax transparency* the *loss pass-through*, and this is still in tact. This means that for tax purposes an S-corporation is treated like a partnership. All losses, as well as profits are passed through to the shareholders in proportion to their interest.

New corporate tax rates make the subject of U.S. corporations something that needs to be carefully considered. There may not be as many specific tax advantages. However, if you do not use the corporation as we describe it, in many cases there will be little tax advantage. The U.S. tax committees of Congress are always looking for ways to neutralize the effect of working under the structure of a corporation, as opposed to an individual sole proprietorship. With the election of each new Congress we must look at the effect changes they will propose in the tax laws will effect our business operations.

One of the most obvious advantages of corporate activity is the 1986 Tax Reform Act (TRA '86). Under TRA '86, deductions for interest payments are reduced or eliminated for individuals. This is not true of corporations. Interest is considered one of the costs of doing business and is therefore a deductible expense. This creates many new strategies with regard to purchasing and owning certain corporate assets for personal use.

Limited Partnerships

In the 1960's and early 1970's the use of limited partnerships by real estate developers were abused. This caused a major problem that leads people to look at this entity with a doubtful eye. The entity is still available and remains a very profitable business entity today. A limited partnership has the advantage of limited liability for the investors or limited partners and leaves all management under the direction of the general partner. This is a very valuable option if the general partner only holds 2% interest in the total structure.

Limited partnership interests can be held by foreign entities. In all cases, any distribution from the partnership is passed on to those with the partnership interest. The distribution is accounted for with a K-1 Form. This would mean that if there was a distribution made to you as an investor in the limited partnership you would need to file a K-1 Form with a 1040 Form for personal taxes. The foreign owner of partnership interest will also receive his proportionate share of the distribution along with the K-1. However, unless a tax form is filed with the United States government, this K-1 income need not be acknowledged.

A common cousin to the Limited Partnership is the Family Limited Partnership (FLP). You need to understand that structurally and practically the entities are identical. The only difference is that the limited partners of the FLP are direct family members. The general partner is completely responsible for the assets of the partnership. The limited partners are protected by the Uniform Limited Partnership laws. Foreign entities can own a minority holding in a FLP without jeopardizing the advantages. Be careful not to abuse the FLP provision. Abuse could lead to the government disallowing the tax advantages that are present with the set up of the FLP.

These tax advantages include the right to place property into the partnership as an exchange for partnership interest treated as an estate planning tool. There would be no tax on this transaction and the basis on the property would pass to the FLP. This potential capital gain could then be gifted to your children as follows.

One of the best uses of the FLP is to gift to your children, who are also limited partners, limited partnership interests. The children limited partners can receive limited partnership interests equal to the limitations of the tax law to exclude any gift taxes. For example, each year you and your spouse could gift up to $40,000.00 in value of partnership interests to your two children. The total amount allocated without gift tax to you or any tax to them.

49

The law allows gifts of $10,000 per person to each recipient. In time, all of the value assets in the FLP could be gifted to the other limited partners (your children) leaving you with only the 2% general partnership interest **while retaining complete responsibility of the assets** and very limited liability. This is a good and effective way to avoid the problems of estate taxes without giving up any power. The FLP is the best asset protection tool. It has no equal.

A judgment creditor with any claim against the limited partner can be granted the right to file a *charging order* against the partnership. In no case will the court require the dissolution of the partnership in order to protect the other partners. The holder of the charging order would have the rights to any distribution made to the member whose assets he had claim to, however, it probably would be a cold day in hell before any distribution was ever made after that time.

To add insult to injury, the judgment creditor is forced to recognize the income he should have received as actually received and would need to declare that amount and pay tax on it as if he had actually received it. If I were the judgment creditor in that position, I would probably sue the attorney for malpractice who filed the charging order in my "behalf".

Limited Liability Company

At the International Tax Planning Association Conference, in the Caribbean in the fall of 1992, those attending were given a very valuable introduction to this new type of business entity that will be used more frequency in the future. The Limited Liability company has all the desirable characteristics of the S-Corporation, the General Partnership or Limited Partnership without the need to attach liability to any single member or class of membership. That is there are no general partners. All of the members are identical and are each held to be limited in liability. Additionally, there is no restriction on ownership of partnership interests by foreign individuals or entities. These advantages make this a very good tool for foreign investors who wish to make use of United States security and real estate advantages, while at the same time enjoying the pass through of gains to the foreign or individual non-liable partner.

The Nevada or Delaware Corporation

International financial and business consultants rarely think of the United States as a useful offshore jurisdiction. However, there are circumstances that dictate the need to look at specific U.S. jurisdictional laws to find a favorable situation for certain international transactions. In those cases, the United States can be an outstanding offshore jurisdiction.

Among these circumstances are certain business ventures that can benefit from U.S.-based operations and the holding of U.S. real property or other assets. In order to gain resident status within the U.S., the use of domestic corporate structures is useful. We need to always look for the best domestic jurisdiction for a corporation as well.

The United States of America and the organization of 12 mature functioning countries into the EC/EU have some similarities. Both organizations are formed as a federation of independent colonies or states. Just as individual states within the United States have certain rights and laws that pertain only to those states; the same sort of autonomy holds true for the individual countries within the EC/EU. Each separate state passes its own laws and regulates its own business activities.

Historically, as the country grew advantages were offered to business by the state of Delaware, which created a business climate that attracted many of the newly formed corporate entities during the Industrial Revolution. It is estimated that at least half of the companies that make up the Fortune 500 list are corporations that were originally chartered in Delaware. This is probably more a factor of historical timing than of real tax or corporate business advantages.

The men and women who tamed the western frontier were individualists who believed strongly in personal freedom and the ideas of personal and business privacy. Unlike Delaware, where corporate structure offered only favorable tax laws, privacy and the sanctity of business records are also written into the laws of western states like Nevada. The business laws of the state of Nevada are the best in the country.

As these western states one-by-one joined the United States, better business opportunities presented themselves. To the U.S. citizen as well as the foreigner, either individual or corporate, the business opportunities of the West are still among the best in the nation. There seems to continue to be an independent spirit in the West. The first IRS sanctioned Limited Liability company law was in the state of Wyoming. The people of the state of Nevada as late as 1990 voted once again not to have reciprocity with the federal government on exchange of tax information.

6
Nevada Corporations

Nevada Corporations as Holding Companies

Some of the midwestern states have provisions in their state constitutions or in statutes passed years ago that forbid foreign ownership of real property, especially farm land. Additionally, the 1986 Tax Reform Act (TRA '86) generally requires all real estate transactions be reported to the federal government. The TRA '86 also requires a tax be withheld at the source, if the payment was to a foreign entity or individual, to cover the tax on any potential profit.

In most cases interstate corporate ownership of property does not fall into the foreign category. Many states treat corporate ownership from another state as domestic for practical purposes. Investors are finding that one of the best ways for them to hold title to property anywhere in the United States is through the use of an incorporated holding company established in the state of Nevada.

If a particular property is held as a corporate asset, and it is the only asset listed on the corporate books, it might be a smart strategy to sell the stock in the corporation to the potential buyer rather than to sell the property itself. The new stockholder could elect himself or herself president of the corporation and do whatever they wanted with the corporate asset, the property. Investors are finding this a viable way to buy and sell their confidential interest in real estate while they keep the profits from the private sale of unlisted corporate stock outside, in a jurisdiction that offers the greatest tax advantage.

States such as California requires a reassessment of real property each time it changes hands. The use of corporate stock in property transactions creates a circumstance where the real property itself does not change hands. The seller can essentially avoid the reassessment as well as a tax on the profit of the sale.

Nevada Stock can be "Bearer Stock"

Clearly, a private holding company works best in a jurisdiction where the stockholders of the corporation are not recorded in any official registry. The state of Nevada offers that opportunity. It is noteworthy that in Nevada the stockholders are unlisted. This makes Nevada corporate stock, bearer stock for all practical purposes.

Nevada state code also creates other advantages related to corporate shares. Stockholders are not required to be U.S. citizens. Their identity is not a matter of public record and they may appoint others to act on behalf of the corporation. Stockholders in Nevada therefore become anonymous. Nevada corporations may issue stock for labor, services, personal property, or real estate, including leases and options.

The board of directors may determine the value of any of these transactions and the decision is final. Stockholders and directors of Nevada corporations are not required to live or hold meetings in Nevada. They are free to act anywhere in the world. A single individual may act as president, secretary, treasurer, and director of a Nevada corporation, thereby fulfilling all disclosure requirements.

Nevada state law requires that any corporation established in the state have a registered agent for service of documents. The corporate registered agent could also contract to maintain the minute book and fulfill the requirements with regard to the listing the officers of the corporation with the secretary of state. Some corporate service centers in the state offer a more complete service, as outlined below.

Nevada as a Business Address

Many business operations in the United States have seen the advantages of Nevada operations. Among them are Citibank credit card processing and many foreign business operations such as Porsche of North America. Some of the advantages are that Nevada has no inventory tax, freight forwarding and warehousing are big business operations in the state.

Domestic or foreign small-business operators are finding that a corporate entity based in the United States offers them special advantages in dealing with the customers who will be the ultimate users of their products or services.

Among these advantages are convenience to the market and the perception of a domestic company, in the minds of those who would limit or exclude foreign competition with domestic products.

There is no minimum capital required to establish a business operation in Nevada. In fact, Nevada has no state corporate taxes, no state personal income tax, no franchise tax, no tax on corporate shares, and no succession tax. It is the most tax-free state in the United States. Clearly, any individual whose business function is that of a consultant or independent contractor offering his services to individuals or companies in any state of the union, would be at an advantage to establish his company as a Nevada corporation and thus takes advantage of this low tax state.

This example illustrates the effect of having no state tax:

If a person or corporation were to establish a business in the High Sierras on the shores of magnificent Lake Tahoe, he or she would find that the state line between California and Nevada goes directly through the lake. Businesses established in a community on the East, or Nevada side of the lake pays no state tax. If the West or California side were the business site, it would be subject to a 9.7% tax on corporate profits.

As with all states, companies in Nevada are subject to the federal tax code. So each corporation is required to file an annual corporate tax form with the federal government. However, it is possible through careful structuring of transactions to upstream much of the potentially taxable profit to its foreign parent or stockholder, without subjection to U.S. withholding.

LAD Financial Services

This author would be amiss in his duties if he outlined the advantages of the Nevada corporation and did not advise the reader of ways to access this information in more detail, or to take advantage of the company formation services we offer. As stated earlier, each state requires that a resident agent represent the company within the state. There are many resident agents in the state of Nevada. Some offer more complete services than others. As a service to its domestic and international clients, LAD Financial Services operates an international corporate consulting service out of our home office in Reno, Nevada. Through this, we make the Nevada corporation accessible to individuals or businesses worldwide and enable our clients to operate the corporate entity for the benefit of the stock-holder in a manner that will comply with Nevada and U.S. law.

Services Include:

1. A company formation within 7 to 10 days.

2. Issuance of a corporate kit that contains all the necessary documentation.

3. Corporate shares.

4. Corporate seal.

5. Articles of incorporation.

6. Organizational minutes that meet the needs of the client.

This is first accomplished by working directly with companies or individuals whom LAD Financial Services know and have confidence in to accomplish the set-up and site management of the client's company structure.

Ongoing Services Include:

1. Oversight and management of the Nevada resident agent.

2. Preparation of semi-annual updated minutes.

3. Preparation by a CPA and filing of necessary corporate tax forms.

4. Filing and recording all necessary documents with the state of Nevada.

5. Maintenance of corporate records.

6. Operations of a remote office for the client.

The Contract for a Remote Office

Many companies in Nevada offer corporate clients an office management contract that includes, among other things, a mailing address, fax forwarding, telephone answering, and other services designed to create a proper business address and presence in the state of Nevada. These services are essential to the client who wishes to set up a foreign office operation on a limited level for any of the reasons outlined above.

The ownership of real property or the remote operation of a business enterprise each should be represented by an actual office presence. The cost of this service is minor when compared to the cost of full corporate office operations. Proper business licenses are obtained and posted, telephones are installed and answered as directed by the corporate officer in charge, and mail is handled according to specific instructions.

Essentially, a turn-key corporate office is established that will allow the client to operate their business endeavor without being concerned about the propriety of the corporate structure. A full-service contract would include a local bank account and arrangements where the required fees of service charged directly to the company account.

Most international business and tax consultants look for ways to legally structure business activities for individuals from high-tax countries wishing to do business in another country. As consultants, LAD Financial Services' objective is to reduce or eliminate the unnecessary expenses imposed by laws in the specific jurisdiction involved.

There are times or circumstances that make it necessary for LAD Financial Services to look at the options that are available within the high-tax country. LAD Financial Services takes advantage of these internal tax laws to structure the domestic or foreign investor or business person in such a way that he or she can produce the highest return on their business investment.

We have shown that such an opportunity exists in the state of Nevada within the United States. Not only is Nevada the best domestic state for business for the U.S. citizen, but it offers important opportunities for access to the U.S. market to the foreign business person or investor as well.

We have also clearly shown that a company structured in the United States should have a physical presence. That presence is set up as a serviced remote office with an address, phone, and a business license in the state where there is a very favorable business climate. If such a company was established, it is best managed by a resident agent who offers more than just an address for service of documents.

If you are planning to use a general business corporation in the U.S., you should consider the Nevada jurisdiction as a corporate site. If you do not now have a corporation, or if you are in a high-tax jurisdiction, you should seriously consider a Nevada corporation.

Utilize the information in "How and Why Americans Go Offshore" to upstream your potential profit to this low-tax state. LAD Financial Services, through its offices in Reno, Nevada, is a business consultant who can assist you in setting up and using your Nevada corporation.

7
Corporate Ownership

Ownership and Value of the Corporation

Personal Ownership

> Most stock in corporations both foreign or domestic is owned by individuals. It is the most common way we participate in business activities while protecting our personal assets from liabilities. Stocks can also be owned in other ways.

Corporate Ownership and Dividend Exclusion

- Stock in C-corporations can be owned by other corporations.

- Stocks in S-corporations are never owned by foreign corporations, whether foreign or domestic.

- There is a U.S. tax dividend exclusion that makes much of the income earned from the subsidiary tax-free. At the very least, your tax on profits that are passed up to the parent corporation will be greatly reduced.

Trust Ownership

Stocks in corporations are owned by trusts, both foreign and domestic. This is an important consideration if you were to establish an asset protection trust in a safe jurisdiction as the Isle of Man and you also wanted to hold the stock to other various corporations in trust.

International Corporate Ownership

Stock in a domestic corporation may be held by a foreign corporation. This makes it possible to upstream potential profit between a corporation in a low-tax state like Nevada to one in a no-tax state like the Isle of Man. Many foreign international jurisdictions offer the same or similar list of advantages as a Nevada corporation, with one important addition. They are outside the U.S. tax jurisdiction so there is no federal tax liability.

In the event stock in the domestic corporation is held by a foreign corporation, it is necessary to take into consideration the tax laws regarding U.S.-source income when transferring funds to the corporate parent. The transfer can be done, but must be done through a company that is established in a country with a bilateral tax treaty with the United States.

Stock Owned by a Family Limited Partnership

The Family Limited Partnership is one of the best asset protection tools available to the U.S. citizen. No business person concerned with protection of assets from lawsuits or government plunder should be without one. Corporate stock, both foreign and domestic, is an asset that is often placed into the body of a family limited partnership. It is also possible to make the foreign corporation the general partner in a family limited partnership.

Use of the Balance Sheet and Profit-and-Loss Statement

It is not possible to understand the concept of up streaming without at least a rudimentary knowledge of the two most important business statements. These are the *balance sheet* and the *statement of profit and loss.*

A balance sheet is a snapshot in time. It tells the financial status of the business on a certain date. It is generally dated at the year end or quarter end and is an essential tool to determine the health of a business.

A statement of profit-and-loss is a history of actions over time. This document covers a defined period, always containing the words "for period ending...." The statement of profit-and-loss records the income and expenses of a business over time. In the United States and in other jurisdictions that use generally accepted accounting principles, your taxes are based on the *bottom-line* profit.

Given this, a smart strategy would be to increase the expenses of a corporation in a high-tax state. To achieve this, interact with a solely owned corporation, a corporation directly or indirectly influenced by or directed by an individual in a low or no tax state. Taxes can be based on the gross profit at the end of a 12-month period. You must be aware of the corporate year end, usually the calendar year. However, C-corporations can still determine their own fiscal years. This is important because of the financial interplay between corporations.

Everything is backwards in a closely held corporation. You are directly affected by the benefits the corporation provides. Don't cut expenses if they have gone toward your personal benefit. Look for ways to mix business with pleasure! So be alert to moving profit above the line and look for expenses that will decrease the dollars that normally would fall to the bottom line. Under current U.S. law, every dollar moved above the line saves you 36 cents in federal taxes. When you add in the state tax and any other taxes that Congress will continue to add to our expenses, this could add up to major savings.

Some creative business advisors suggest *red-lining.* This is always putting the corporation into the red. LAD Financial Services does not feel it is best to always red-line the corporation. We suggest that you learn to *gray-line* the profit with just a shade of pink. It is always better to make a little profit and pay a little tax. This will greatly reduce your chances for audit, and if audited you will always fall into the profit--making pile of corporations, even if you only made a few dollars profit.

In order to avoid the problems associated with intercorporate authority, it is important that you transact business in what is called an *arms-length transaction*. You will protect your position best by being sure that all transactions that may involve a problem in the tax area are ratified by the board of directors. Preferably, by a board of directors where you are not in authority. Once the board of directors ratifies the transaction and records it in the minutes, it becomes an action of the corporation and not one directly attributed to you.

The smart owner began reading "How and Why Americans Go Offshore" and, following its advise moved the company to a state corporate tax-free and state personal income tax-free jurisdiction...

8
Maximizing Use of Corporations

"Maximize the use of domestic and foreign corporations for privacy, protection, and profit."

A Corporation is Not Good if it is Not Used

It is not uncommon to see doctors and other small-business operators who have formed professional or closely held small business corporations for the sole purpose of providing a structure for the pension and profit-sharing plans we discussed earlier. This is a serious mistake. A corporation is like another person. A person who likes to be used. It wants to be a part of the deal.

Every deal has at least two participants. When you serve on the board of directors of a corporation, you are in a position to deal. You can make deals with the corporation. Deals that will have a benefit for you as an individual, as well as for the entity you are using on the other side of the deal.

The Components of Cost

Whenever a deal is made, both the buyer and the seller agree on a fair and equitable price. No transaction takes place without that agreement. Every transaction has at least two factors that make up the cost involved.

13. The first factor is made up of cost of material and the mark-up, the cost of a service and the value we place on it, or even the cost of the use of money, which we call interest.

14. The second factor is the mark-up that we call the potential profit.

If you are in a "powerful position of influence," on the board of directors of two different corporations that do business with each other, you have some influence on the components of cost. You are in a position to move money between the two corporations. Money is best moved on the backs of product, service, or interest. Depending on the decision you make, money can easily flow from a high-tax state to a low-tax state, or indeed from a country that is high-tax to a country that does not tax its business entities.

So it is important to look at the tax exposure of the two companies to see which corporation is best suited to make the most profit. Our government as well as many others in the world base taxation on the profit made at the end of the year.

A Little About Deductibility

In the U.S. people who are aware of the tax implications of their action are always concerned about deductibility. They ask, "Is it deductible?" before any expenditure is made. It should be noted that the word "deductibility" is only relevant to taxes. Essentially, it increases allowable expenses against potentially taxable income. In other words, in the course of doing business you move bottom-line potential profit above the line to an item to be expensed. It is noteworthy at this point that if the corporation has no potential tax, or if it is set up in a jurisdiction with no potential tax on its income, the word and the concept of deductibility are of no concern...it is irrelevant.

Tax Strategies

It should be noted, once again, that the primary purpose for international involvement is not to avoid taxes. Though this is an important side effect of a carefully designed plan it should not be our only consideration. We are in business to make a profit, and to earn a greater profit than our competitor.

Taxes are one of the greatest costs to operations of a business. This is true in the United States, France, Germany, England and certainly Nordic Sweden and Denmark. The selection of the proper entity and the proper jurisdiction will enhance our ability to reduce costs and thus earn a greater potential profit. So, careful planning involving tax exposure is an important consideration.

Every foreign organization should have at least one entity formed in a jurisdiction with maximum tax advantage. This could be thought of as the organizations "piggy bank." It is into this entity that all profits of the organization would eventually flow. The key to corporate tax strategy is to make the most profit in the corporation that is established in the jurisdiction with the lowest tax exposure.

Since you are in a "powerful position of influence," on the board of directors of entities in both high- and low-tax jurisdictions, you can make decisions that impact on the potential after-tax profit. A properly selected foreign jurisdiction can be tax-free. Our job as a business consultant is to search the world to find the best possible location for your business venture, so that you can earn and retain the maximum return on your corporate investments.

It should also be noted that if the business entity is properly structured the business purpose must only meet the terms of the company bylaws in the jurisdiction of its domicile. That is to say, that if the company with which you work is properly designed and created it can be a foreign investment company and in no way run up against the United States tax laws with regard to such entities.

The Publishing Company

A common example of a foreign entity bestowing a very positive tax advantage is of a foreign publishing company. Most of the newsletter writers that I have known in the United States use an offshore publishing company in order to divert potentially taxable profit. If this company is properly structured so the U.S. citizen has no beneficial interest, but holds only a "powerful position of influence" as a minority member of the board of directors, he or she is in a position to build a very profitable offshore business.

Assume the individual is a writer and writes a book. The author then sells the manuscript to the publisher for a small fee. He or she must declare the fee as income and pay the appropriate tax. The publisher, in turn, converts the manuscript into a marketable book. The publisher may use the services of the writer and of course will interact with the writer constantly throughout the publishing process. When the book is ready for distribution and sale, the publishing company may contract or sell the book either directly to the end user or to a distributing company. In either case, the publisher sells the book for very near the list price.

You, the author, as a prudent international business person, may choose to become a distributor and to buy your book and distribute it in the United States. You would pay dearly for the product. Such a transaction would move a considerable amount of money to the offshore publishing company. This profit would be retained offshore, tax-free, until such a time as you as an influential member of that board of directors votes to use it in a personal beneficial way.

How to Maximize
Your Personal Involvement

We find today that the vast majority of our clients are individuals who either already have a business generating international income or are seriously considering expanding their business to the world market. This is, of course, the ideal situation. A company that is established as a subsidiary of a domestic corporation would need to report its income to the federal government.

However, if the structure was one that accomplished the same function but was not connected to the domestic corporation, it could be looked at as a totally foreign entity and would be treated differently from both an earnings and taxation standpoint.

Another group of our clients is interested in forming a foreign corporation to start a new business venture and wants to be sure that the structure complies with U.S. law and will not jeopardize the U.S. citizen if he or she is involved in some way with the operation of the business. These individuals see great opportunity to develop a good thriving business, but they are immediately concerned with regard to how they get to share in the benefits of this success.

Finally, we have a substantial number of clients who understand the system and are seeking complete privacy in their foreign affairs. These people are without a doubt in the best possible position by becoming involved with our system and reaping the benefits from its use.

How to Get Money in and out of Your Corporation

The most often asked question of people who are considering the use of foreign structures is "How do we transfer money to a foreign company?" To be honest in today's world, getting money into the United States is considerably easier than getting it out.

Drug laws have created monitoring systems that are very invasive of your private affairs. The U.S. government feels it can only solve the problem of drugs by tracking the flow of money out of the United States. They have therefore put stringent reporting requirement in place on banks and financial institutions and on individuals as well.

To get money out, you might first consider the idea of a private annuity to the corporation as a way to place funds under its direction for your eventual benefit, without actually taking title or possession of any stock. This concept will be discussed in more detail in another section of this book.

The most common method of getting money into the foreign company is through the use of a loan. This can either be interest free or interest bearing. You, as the lenders are in a position to make that decision. Whatever decision you make it must be substantiated with the proper paperwork and be signed by both the borrower and the lender.

After we have formed your foreign corporation and you have capitalized or funded it with your after-tax dollars as either loans or equity capital, you are ready to make the corporation work for you.

Think of any loan to the corporation as you would "junk bonds." Actually, they are similar and can be treated the same for tax purposes. Junk bonds generally carry a high return, in some cases with no coupon.

The risk is that when the bond comes due, the firm may not be in business or otherwise default on the loan. Present tax law holds that a loan or bond to a business or corporation, as opposed to government bonds, does not generate "phantom income." In such a case, you would not be taxed for money earned but not received. At some point you would take the interest earned on the bonds as income and at that time would declare it and pay the appropriate tax.

How to Get the Money Back

We are always asked at this point, "How do I get to the money when I want it?" This is a proper question and one that will be answered, but first we make very clear three cardinal rules:

• Rule #1: Don't mess with the IRS

When you take constructive receipt of money as salary or dividends, you must declare the income and pay the appropriate tax. As unpopular and unfair as the proposition is, the United States is one of a very few countries that tax its citizens anywhere in the world on their active and passive income. Most other countries tax their resi-

73

dents only. So when you take constructive receipt of money from your corporation, it must be declared as income and the appropriate taxes paid. However, as you will later see, it is not always necessary to take constructive receipt.

- Rule #2: It is within the normal rules and procedures of business corporations to provide certain benefits to their key employees, directors, and officers.

This would also include the managing consultant upon whose advice the company places much confidence. It should be clear by now that using a corporation as an ongoing business entity offers a large number of perquisites or benefits that are not construed as constructive receipt. Our main goal is to maximize your indirect personal benefits in the domestic corporation. Pass off to the foreign corporation any benefits that may be questioned here. Don't try to fight the system. Pay for things that can cause you headaches with money that is already out of the system and is tax-free.

If you serve on the board of directors or are a consultant to the foreign corporation, this is not a problem. You can lend your influence on both boards of directors. If you are appointed to the position of managing consultant or director, it is your responsibility to make those kinds of decisions for the corporation. In-as-much as these are general business decisions, they generally do not need board ratification.

To the best of our knowledge there is no form or report within the federal government that requires you to list the jobs, positions, or responsibilities you may have in business ventures anywhere in the world. You do have to list the income you are paid from those activities, but you are not required to list the position if it is unpaid.

- Rule #3: It is the fiduciary responsibility of the board of directors and officers of any corporation, domestic or foreign, to invest the excess corporate funds such as to produce the highest possible return to the stockholders.

This is universally true no matter what the corporate jurisdiction or who is the beneficiary of the stock in the corporation. Remember, it is your duty, even if your heirs or trusts are the stockholders.

The "Super IRA", Using Corporate Structure

Remember before the 1986 tax law, when as U.S. citizens we had the option to invest our money in Individual Retirement Accounts (IRA) with important tax advantages? We think of the foreign corporation as the ultimate IRA, the International Retirement Account. Unlike the U.S. IRAs there are no maximum deposits and no penalties for early withdrawal. Earnings are compounded until withdrawn and are not subject to taxes. Of course, any time you withdraw the earnings and take constructive receipt of the money in the U.S. you must declare the income and pay the appropriate tax.

If your business entity meets what we call the IRS "Tetra Test" (see Chapter 10), nothing needs to be reported to anyone except to the international corporate board of directors. You are an employee, or a consultant of a business that is not under the jurisdiction of the United States. Generally, in most offshore business havens, information required by the board of directors is made clear to the employee and once given to them this is as far as the information goes. Your board of directors will determine the need to report regarding withdrawal of funds.

How to Operate the
Corporate Bank Account

Most individuals who become involved in foreign companies or trusts find that because of the lack of the need to report income and pay tax having a personal account is unnecessary. As the managing consultant they can take advantage of their position and request the company administrator to spend the money in the company accounts in certain ways at any time.

There is a great deal of confusion about the need to report your signature power on the corporate bank account. Some say this is required, others say it is not. We have found that after our clients have developed a working relationship with the administrator of the company or trust they no longer feel the need to have any signature control of the company accounts.

It is possible, even preferable, to set up the corporate account in such a way that you do not have signature power, but still have management authority over corporate disbursements. This is called acknowledgment and is commonly asked for by foreign bankers. In any case, you need to remember that it is not your account, so you have no need to report its activity.

As a corporate officer, you may be given mandate power to re-allocate the corporate assets. This means that by letter or fax you can direct the bank to re-allocate its cash assets into another asset form. You could select any number of different types of assets. You might favor certificates of deposit, mutual funds, real estate, or even U.S. Treasury notes. You are limited only by your imagination.

It is in your best interest to use the services of a foreign–based independent business consultant. London is still the financial crossroads of the world. By using the services of an offshore business administrator like Intercon Associates, your interaction with the foreign corporation will have a London administration office, with secretarial and mailing services.

Establishing and Using
a Corporate Line of Credit

Corporations generally need and use large amounts of money. It is not uncommon for a corporation to request a line of credit from its bank to hold in operating reserve. It may be necessary for the corporate directors to submit their financial statements to the bank expected to grant the line of credit. This is normal banking procedure.

Also, it is not uncommon to personally guarantee a corporate loan if your personal statement is very good. In some cases it may be good to use your property as security for a line of credit on the corporate account. If, after all, you insist on having a personal account it is best to have both your corporate and personal accounts at the same bank to maximize the use of the credit line. Later, as your corporate assets grow, you will diversify your bank accounts as well.

We always give the bank officer the right to transfer funds between accounts so that your personal account will never go over the $10,000 reporting threshold. You can always account for this transaction as a loan between you and the corporation. A $25,000 line of credit on your personal account, as well as a corporate line of $250,000 is not out of line, especially if your corporation has a healthy balance sheet. This should cover the reasonable purchases of a prudent international business person.

9
Upstreaming:
Corporate Interaction

"Upstreaming is the key to moving money"

Methods of Upstreaming

Intercorporate Billing

The most common mean of upstreaming is for one company to bill another for certain proper business expenses. What is an expense to one business will be income to the business that receives the payment. If you are in a "powerful position of influence," either on the board of directors or as a consultant to the board of directors of both corporations, you can have some effect on the flow of money through the payment of these legitimate bills.

We, LAD Financial Services, recommend billing for services of key people, such as those in accounting and in management. This will include consultant services provided by stockholders. The concept of upstreaming applies to all companies both domestic and foreign.

One of the most common upstreaming techniques is billing for supplies, manufactured goods, or for the lease of furnishings or buildings. The corporation in the low-tax state holding title to property can write a lease to the corporation in the high-tax state that will drain nearly all of its ready cash.

A common collection technique is factoring accounts. This is when the provider of the goods or service discounts their bill and turns it over to another corporation for collection. This is a common foreign function. It is not uncommon to discount a bill by 30% to 40%. If you are involved with the collection corporation as well, you can see a rapid transfer of 30% to 40% of the potential profit. In the offshore world, a considerable amount of business transactions comes from re-invoicing for goods and services through a company that may factor those accounts.

Intercorporate Loans

Corporations borrow money. This is a common way to meet ongoing corporate expenses. If a subsidiary corporation needs to float a loan from its parent, or from any other corporation for that matter, the two negotiate a rate of interest and make the deal. Though the interest rate is generally up to the lender, if you are involved on both sides of the deal, you will probably be more willing to pay a higher rate of interest in order to move money to the company in the low tax state.

Nevada is a state where there are no usury laws, so the interest rate can be very high. Certain foreign jurisdictions also have no usury laws. Any time a loan is made, the documents must be signed and recorded in the minutes of both corporations. It is important that the transaction be a normal business transaction. This can create a "mountain of debt." A prudent business person who has loaned money to a corporation in any other jurisdiction will want some sort of security. This may be the equipment, buildings, or vehicles that are owned by the borrowing corporation.

In the United States, when an individual or corporation loans money, the property or asset used as security is evidenced by an UCC1 form. This form is filed with the secretary of state and takes precedence over all other creditors in the case of a judgment. This gives the lender great security. At the same time, it also provides a way to transfer large amounts of capital to another corporate entity, in case of failure of the borrower to repay the debt.

Intercorporate Securities

Since it is common for corporations to own the stock of other corporations, the dependent corporation may be required to transfer a certain amount of its potential gross profit to the parent corporation for management services rendered.

Maximizing Personal Benefits

It is normal in business and recognized by any government that the costs of doing business are deductible from the gross income. This includes general and administrative expenses, which can be loaded with personal benefits. Remember, the bottom line is taxed. So the object is to move some of that potentially taxable money up into the expense area and at the same time enjoy the effect of that expenditure. In all cases, it is imperative that the secretary keeps accurate records. Enter all major transactions in the minutes. As a rule, whatever the board of directors votes to do it can do, but it must be documented by entering it into the minutes.

81

The Charles J. Givens organization out of Altamonte Springs, Florida, through its educational forums offer many creative and viable strategies for maximizing your personal profit by creating legitimate tax deductible expenses. Joining this organization and taking advantage of the seminars, books and programs they offer will bring instant and incredible returns. In many cases it is possible to buy your car, your home, your uniform as a business expense. If you are always alert to the possibility, most of the things you do can in some way be related to a business venture, and is therefore a deductible expense.

These may not always be good business decisions. That's O.K. The government cannot pass laws requiring you to make good decisions. They can require you to record those decisions if you intend to use them to reduce your tax exposure. Don't make the mistake of claiming large items that will flag the interest of the screening officer at the IRS. You are not interested in attracting attention, only enjoying the benefits without being harassed.

Spread the big-ticket items between corporations. Since each corporation files its own tax form, an item that might attract attention can be claimed in part on more than one tax form. Don't try to be greedy and claim more than 100%. If you are audited and found out this is fraud. Be aware that tax forms are sent to different regional offices and chances of bringing them all together are remote. It is hard to match up all the parts of a multi-corporate empire. The Nevada corporation tax forms go to Ogden, Utah; Northern California tax forms go to Fresno; yours may go anywhere else.

Under TRA '86, an individual can no longer deduct all of his or her personal interest expense. This is not true of corporations. This expense is still a legitimate business deduction. So if you are going to buy a car on credit be sure it is the corporate car and not your personal car. Pay for it out of the corporate account and deduct the interest as a business expense.

Anything that is subject to question in the United States with regard to taxes can be purchased by a foreign corporation. This can act for your benefit without regard to tax aspects, because the foreign corporation is not subject to taxation. No one audits these corporate tax forms.

Use of Business or Tax Havens— Why and for How Long

As long as free people in a civilized world can do business with each other, there will be a need for and provision made for tax-free business havens. Imagine four business people in a plane traveling across the Atlantic. While standing around the galley in the middle of the night, they hit on a good idea for a business venture. They decide to go ahead. They must decide what country to use to establish the corporation. No single one of them wants to have it based in his or her country for tax reasons, so they choose a neutral country where nonresident aliens can establish corporations with no applicable tax.

That is the simple basis for business and tax havens. This freedom to go into business will not soon disappear. Also, one only has to look at the foreign investment in the United States. Foreign nationals have been buying big portions of our U.S. assets. This is an important element of international currency exchange. It brings our dollars back to our soil.

The 1983 U.S. tax law contained one very important element. The withholding of U.S.-source income tax from foreign investors was quietly eliminated. This will not be reinstated. The Clinton administration, though struggling with the enormous debt and looking for ways to increase income, will not do anything that would impact on the foreign source of bailout money. National economics preclude change. Try to imagine what would happen to the world's economy if the United States once again withheld tax on Japan's investment in our U.S. Bonds or T-bills.

We are concerned that "foreigners" are buying up America. In fact, over 80% of the investment made in American assets is in the form of stock in American business. You too, can share in that buying opportunity if you create a foreign artificial person, the foreign corporation.

How to Be a One Person Multi-National

There is nothing inherent in the laws of business that says only "big business" can be multinational. It is possible for a small business to be multinational as well. Size is not the determining factor. It is possible to live in one country, bank in a second country, work in a third country, and invest in other countries. You can earn your income from a fourth country, set up your corporate office in a fifth country, etc. We live in a relatively free country and are not limited in business options.

84

Interface with the Foreign Corporation

If you enjoy international travel, establish a foreign tour company or be a consultant to an international educational program that requires your presence. If you take a small salary, declare it and pay the tax. If you are concerned about the deduction of the costs of your international travel, be sure to show some income. It will attract attention if you only show a loss for your international business activity. Do not try to deduct the costs without declaring the income. If you have set up a company to contract out your service and expertise and if that company is a foreign one, you need never see the income. It can be paid directly to your foreign corporation.

In this case, the foreign corporation would prepay your costs and you would show no deductions nor income on your personal or domestic corporate tax forms. In as much as the U.S. tax system looks with such disfavor upon the notion of a spouse accompanying you on your business trip, it might be advisable to have the foreign corporation pay all of those expenses and in that manner avoid the problem of explanation as to the spouse's purpose on the trip.

85

Notes:

10

Types of International Businesses

Establishing Your International Business

Examples of International Business

Throughout this book we give examples and more detail in the various types of business ventures that lend themselves to foreign structure. We have heard it said that one should think of anything you want to do, then ask yourself: "Where in the world is the best place to do this?"

Import and Export

One of most common types of business that lends itself to foreign incorporation is that of import and export. The United States imports billions more than it exports. These are money transactions that can occur outside the boundary of the United States.

At one time, in conjunction with LaVera Tours, Ltd., we imported new Mercedes-Benz and Porsche cars. There was a good market at the time. It added a special twist to the tour business. This enabled each doctor on the tour to use his or her own new car as ground transportation during the two-week educational safari. We imported a lot of cars. If the dollar is upside down, it might be better to export Chevy Camaros to Germany. The kids love them. This is only one of the many things that can be transferred profitably between countries.

Consider for a moment the effect of a foreign company in the chain of businesses involved in the automobile transaction. What would happen if you sold the Chevy's first to an offshore company at little or no profit, that could then resell them at a very high price to a dealer in Germany? Can you see where the profit would remain?

Also, if that offshore company was established in a jurisdiction that did not tax its companies owned by non-residents or offered tax free incentives to set up the business there the profits would simply compound with time and grow to become a very successful enterprise.

Finally, if your relationship with that company was such that it provided you with certain life style benefits or loans for investment capital upon your suggestion, can you see where you could have some real benefits from this transaction?

One of the best companies that lends itself to a foreign structure is an international tour company operated by a domestic travel agency. This is the model of LaVera Tours, Ltd. In this case, your foreign company collects from the traveling client the full marked-up cost of the travel package. It then pays your local travel company only enough to cover the fixed costs of the travel package, leaving all the mark-up and profit in the accounts of the foreign tour company.

Another common example is the publishing business. If you are a writer, anything you write can be written on contract to a foreign company. The foreign publishing company can then sell the finished product to your retail bookstore in the U.S. at whatever price you are willing to pay. Think about it...write your manuscript for very little and have your bookstore pay dearly for the end product. On the back of your book a considerable amount of money could be moved to your foreign publishing company.

Doctors or others subject to malpractice or liability lawsuits may be interested in setting up a captive foreign insurance company that reinsures them through Lloyds of London or one of the dozens of reinsured companies, and creates a foreign investment company by design. In another section of this book we go into the captive insurance concept in detail and use a company, International Indemnity Insurance Company, as an example of a company that would take advantage of all of the international tax planning and asset protection expertise as well as that of liability protection.

It is the proper function of the insurance company to collect the premium, no matter how large, and to pay the claim, no matter how small, and then to invest the excess capital in the corporate treasury for the benefit of the stockholders, no matter who they may be. It may also take advantage of the many international tax laws that exist to offer the policy holders many other perks and advantages not available to them in domestic insurance schemes.

Often, we are asked if it's possible to simply establish a foreign investment company. The tax law specifically names foreign investment companies as entities with which a U.S. citizen cannot be involved, if its purpose is tax avoidance. However, if the company is properly structured so that the U.S. citizen shows no beneficial interest, it will not fall under that definition.

If You are a Listed Stockholder of a Foreign Corporation, the Business Must Be Legitimate

The law in the United States does not prohibit citizens from owning stock in foreign corporations. They can own all of the stock if that is their desire. Clearly, if you owned all the stock you would have total power over the corporation and it would fall under the rules of a controlled foreign corporation with the IRS. If you own less than half the stock, you do not have total power over the corporation through stock ownership. There may be other means of total power, and you should be aware of that the IRS would classify the business as a "controlled foreign corporation" in this case as well.

If you own more than 5% of the stock in a public company (or 10% of a non-public corporation), you must file this with the Securities and Exchange Commission (SEC). So, it may not be in your best interest to own any stock in your active corporation. If you own less than half the stock, you must rely on some other way to persuade the board of directors to ratify your business decisions. Additionally, if the active business is an investment or holding company, you must disclose your ownership to the IRS. If this were the case you would do not want to be a stockholder.

Well-informed offshore advisors will suggest to you that the structure used for your business activity is best created in a way that is totally disconnected from you, or from the country in which you reside. The more disconnected it is, the better it will withstand any government or personal challenge.

If You Own Stock,
it Must Clear the IRS "Tetra Test"

There are four business structures that the IRS has specifically set aside as ones that must be disclosed if you are a stockholder. The IRS is aware of U.S. citizens' efforts to

avoid taxes through foreign ownership, and has set up roadblocks to catch the unwary. The applicability of the Accumulated Earnings Tax is the fifth red flag. We call this list the IRS 'Tetra Test".

- PFIC: Passive Foreign Investment Company
- FPHC: Foreign Personal Holding Corporation
- CFC: Controlled Foreign Corporation
- FIC: Foreign Investment Company
- AET: Accumulation Earnings Tax

To Avoid Being Listed, Remember the "Rule of 11"

Less than 50% ownership shows no total power, so the first three structures would be eliminated from consideration here. If you own more than 10%, you must file that information with the IRS. So if you must own stock, you should own less than 10% of the issued shares.

Suppose, the minimum issue would be eleven (11) shares. You would own one share and the balance would be issued to others. These may include nominee stockholders, trusts, other companies, or family and friends. If you get 11 friends together to form a company and attempt to take a proxy to have power over their shares, be aware of the possibility of falling into the controlled foreign corporation (CFC) category.

I like to use the "Bill Gates, my best buddy" example. Suppose Bill Gates, the founder of Microsoft®, were your best friend. Today he is worth 7 billion dollars. He says to you, "Buddy, I have a yacht in the Mediterranean, a Ski Lodge in Aspen, an Island in the Caribbean and anything else you can imagine. If you want to use it all you have to do is ask." Does it really make any difference to you that you do not own or hold title to all these assets?

Remember, you are looking for benefits, not ownership. Holding title to the stock has no intrinsic value. Being in a position to influence the board of directors or the treasurer can offer considerable pleasure; as can the use of the corporate assets for your pleasure, borrowing money at low or no interest, or to arrange a gift to buy yourself a new Mercedes.

Set Up Business In a Jurisdiction with No Corporate Tax

It is essential that your business consultant research the laws and select a jurisdiction where the law allows non-resident aliens to organize companies and be exempt from taxation. There are many tax haven countries that are very well suited for this. New ones are being formed every month, and in our (LAD Financial Services) opinion as long as free people can go into business together there will be places that favor the business they offer.

In Europe some of the outstanding examples are Monaco, Luxembourg, Gibraltar, the Isle of Man, Jersey or Guernsey, and Malta among others. In the Caribbean, in addition to Panama, which offers special advantages, there are the Bahamas, Cayman Islands, Costa Rica, Turks and Caicos, the island of Montserrat and the list go on.

In Appendix I "The Isle of Man: A Business and Tax Haven" we have included a very detailed discourse on the Isle of Man. This is one of the best business and tax havens in the world. It has a thousand-year democracy and is very independent. The language is English and it has excellent communications. We use the Isle of Man as our jurisdiction of first choice. It is possible under the laws of this small island country to set up a company and operate it in a way that will totally protect the members as well as give them the freedom to act as responsible business people.

The Active Corporation
We Call "Level I"

We at LAD Financial Services consider any working foreign business entity, whether it be a bank, insurance company, investment company, or general corporation, to be the active corporation. We designate this Level I. It is important that the Level I company have its active office outside the United States.

Using the services provided by a responsible corporate management firm after they have set up your corporate structure will validate and substantiate your foreign entity. For instance, by contracting with Intercon Associates you can share office space, work through the general corporate administrative office in London, and be able to use that address for all your international business activities. This will provide you with an address, a phone with your listed number, staff support, and an executive office suite for your use when you are in town.

93

This creates essentially a turn-key corporation. You have complete corporate staff support to maintain your corporation in such a way that you can concentrate on managing your business and your wealth. Corporations such as the ones described above are used by many people. They range from tax protesters to people in the White House. Most of us are legitimate business people that fall in between these two extremes.

If you think carefully about the charges that were brought against Oliver North, you will recognize that his corporation was indeed proper. The special prosecutor with all the power of the government could not charge him in that matter. The charges for which he was found guilty were that he lied to Congress, and built a fence to protect himself and his family with money that was presumed to be not his own.

Actually, it appears that his foreign corporation bought surplus missile parts from the U.S. government. These were then sold at a tremendous profit to the Iranians. The profit was kept offshore. The corporation then chose to donate its profit to the Nicaraguan resistance fighters. These are perfectly legal business activities and he could not be charged in that respect.

Out of U.S. Legal and Tax Jurisdiction

There is every reason to believe that a company organized as illustrated previously, even if it was not too successful at its primary business and was temporarily engaged in the investment of excess corporate funds, would not be classified as a foreign investment company. A properly established foreign corporation must be set up and operated in a way that it is outside the tax jurisdiction of the

94

United States. It is also out of reach of the U.S. court system. That's real asset protection.

If the owners of the majority of shares were a foreign asset protection trust, all assets held in the corporate shell would be completely safe from claims and judgments. Since we have been in this business for many years, we have found that most of our clients find that they need nothing more than the level one company. It is usually formed as an Isle of Man guarantee company so it can serve as either a Level I or Level II company for practical purposes.

The Level II Entity

The Isle of Man guarantee company, Panama corporation, or the Liechtenstein anstalt are all Level II entities. There are certain countries that have established business entities that often are used to disguise or obscure ownership. There are many reasons why one may not want to ever show up as the beneficial owner of a business. These reasons may range from the size of that person's wealth to perception of a degree of danger to his or her life. These entities include the Liechtenstein anstalt, the Panama bearer share company, and the Isle of Man company limited by guarantee.

If it is your desire not to show any involvement in an active foreign corporation, it is necessary and possible to structure it in a way to obscure the ownership and still leave you in a "powerful position of influence." As stated above, this is not regularly used. We find that an intermediate company or trust is more often needed because of the possibility of "doing substantial business in the United States" and the need to avoid withholding on U.S.-source income.

Suppose you have established your foreign corporation and, as an officer or advisor to that corporation, have operated it in a manner that has shown a profit. If you have accumulated a large surplus in the treasury, you are confronted with the need to invest the excess profits. You are obligated under the normal rules of business operations to invest these excess funds in a way that will produce the best possible return. This creates the need to look at various international investment opportunities.

11
International Investment Options

The Investment of Corporate Excess Funds

If you continue building a solid business venture, at some point one corporation is going to have a considerable amount of money to invest in a tax-free environment. This is the natural end result of upstreaming, and good management of the foreign company. If you are a director of any corporation or a consultant to the director, your responsibility is to act in a proper business-like way to get the best return on these corporate funds. Remember, it is your fiduciary responsibility to invest the corporate excess funds to generate the highest return possible for the stockholders. As an international investor, you will welcome the assistance of your international investment advisor and business consultant.

The Role of Offshore Investment Advisors

U.S. citizens are slowly waking up to the reality that we are members of a global village. Advances in communication and transportation have reduced the size of the world to something that holds advantages for each of us. This has given rise to a new profession. Several business advisors with knowledge of the international market have expanded their services to include offshore investment for individuals or companies who want to expand their horizons beyond their national borders.

International business advisors deal mostly with the little people or those with assets, free assets are between $100,000 and $10M. These are the forgotten individuals who fall between the cracks, with regard to knowledge of international opportunities. Fortune 500 companies have lawyers and accountants who have made these secrets common knowledge in their board rooms for many years.

After our (LAD Financial Services) clients are advised with regard to the best possible structure for their business activity, we assist the client through our relationship with Intercon Associates to actually set up and administer the company in a turn-key manner. In this environment, clients are free to operate the businesses and manage their own wealth. Understanding the interaction between corporate entities will open many doors and create many legal and proper bridges that you may never have considered previously. This is the role of the offshore investment and business advisor.

Offshore investment advisors are not about always making gigantic returns on your money. They are more often concerned with the safety of what you have and setting up structures and investments that will preserve your capital and allow it to grow undiluted by continuing confiscatory taxation.

The Offshore Institute and the
International Tax Planners Association

At the first Offshore Convention sponsored by Offshore Investment Magazine, June 1989 in London, an organization of offshore advisors and consultants was formed. The name of the organization is the Offshore Institute. One of the institute's primary objectives is to coordinate education and qualifications of international investment business advisors. Being a member, or being associated with a member of the institute carries with it a certain degree of credibility.

To become a member, one must be recognized as competent in the field, have shown ability by practicing for at least six years, and have completed a certain number of hours of advanced education in the field. Members will be able to indicate their proficiency by using the titles of AOI for associate, MOI for master, or FOI for fellow of the Offshore Institute.

In a short time this organization will fill an important and viable need for two important reasons. The first reason is to relieve the pent-up demand for a professional organization within the ranks of offshore advisors. The second reason is to respond to the pressure of the business person, for some way to be assured of competence.

Another important organization for the individual involved in offshore tax planning and transborder transactions is the International Tax Planners Association (ITPA). This organization was founded by Milton Grundy, a British barrister and an internationally recognized authority on tax matters. The ITPA holds meetings in various cities around the world where seminars are offered to over 1000 worldwide members. It is meetings like this that will give the international planner the latest changes and improvements in the field of international tax planning. In selecting your offshore planner one should be careful in dealing with anyone who has not taken the time and paid the price of membership in one or both of these organizations.

Profits in the World Market

Americans have always believed that the sun rises in the Atlantic and sets in the Pacific, and that the rest of the world lives in darkness, or had not yet been discovered. It is hard for us to accept the fact that 77% of world commerce is outside the United States. Much of it is sold to Americans.

For instance, you woke up this morning to the sounds of a Korean alarm clock, ground some Colombian coffee in your German Krups®coffee grinder, read the paper printed on Canadian paper pulp with Korean ink, dressed in your English suit, and Italian shoes, got in your Japanese car, worked all day on your Japanese clone of an IBM® computer and ended the day with a little Irish whiskey.

A lot of today's profit was made on you. Through the effective use of your foreign corporation, you can now share in that profit. You too can sell your product or services to the American people.

Some Investment Options are Reportable, Some are Not

We live in a global village; every person is dependent on the other. There is little left of the Monroe Doctrine. The effect of improvements in electronic communications has opened the world stock and gold markets to a 24-hour cycle.

Even if you are using your personal foreign checking account as access to the international investment market, you should be aware that some investments may fall outside the need-to-report category. These include the purchase of gold and silver, foreign annuity-type life insurance, and certain foreign umbrella mutual funds. Many of the European mutual funds show a far better track record than the best of the American funds.

These umbrella funds, that do not need to be reported, are available to you from a knowledgeable financial planner or international business consultant. Many European money managers have an enviable track record. If it is your wish that the board of directors invest some of its money with these managers, this can easily be arranged. They generally work with large accounts in excess of $50,000.

You can now buy international stock funds from a foreign base. Since this is a foreign corporation investment, there is no need to report the activity in the corporate account. You can invest in international government or corporate bonds, or Euro-bonds through your foreign banker or international business consultant.

International Play with Currency and Interest

As we mentioned earlier, on occasion we switch our entire corporate account to another more favorable currency within the banking system. European banks have held multiple currency accounts for years. We have been able to earn a very good return by this simple technique. American banks have had that option available to them since January 1990. We have heard that very few banks are prepared to handle foreign currency accounts, even though the law will now allow it.

Borrowing money in one currency and depositing it in another is another interesting currency play. Gary Scott, in his book <u>Three Confidential Reports</u> describes it as the currency sandwich. The Danish bank, Janske Bank, has a fund that takes advantage of this opportunity. The object is to borrow funds from a country with low interest costs and deposit funds in a country that pays high interest. At the end of the period, one account is cashed in to pay off the other, allowing the difference to remain in the corporate account.

Reinvestment in America Tax–Free

The Reagan Tax Reduction Act of 1983 created a major shift in the investment options offered to foreign investors. Included in that act was the elimination of the general withholding tax on U.S.-earned income to foreigners. TRA '86 replaced the withholding, but listed many exemptions. This, together with the devaluation of the dollar, following immediately thereafter, has made America one of the world's best tax havens for foreign investors.

This is why the Japanese have purchased a major portion of the national deficit. To them it is an exempt investment. They receive 100% of the earned interest. They realize that a major earthquake could wipe out modern Japan as we know it. They sit on one of the highest peaks on the Pacific "ring of fire." With their money on deposit in the U.S. Treasury, they feel confident in eventual recovery.

It is the British who are the largest foreign investors in American assets. Over 80% of the investments made by foreigners in the American economy is in the form of takeover of American companies. Takeover madness is not limited to Americans; these stocks are available on the open market. When properly structured, your foreign corporation is a "foreigner" and may be able to take advantage of these most-favored laws. In this manner it may be possible for you to "re-invest in America" tax-free.

Investing in International Real Estate

Real estate investments are always a good possibility. If the foreign board of directors chooses, it may invest in real estate anywhere in the world, including in the United States. The U.S. tax law does require a tax withheld on transactions going through escrow, but a knowledgeable business consultant can advise you about ways to effect the transaction without that withholding. One of the best ways is to use the Nevada corporation for ownership of the real estate assets, as outlined earlier.

By using a Nevada corporation to hold title to the real estate, with the stock in the domestic corporation being owned by the foreign corporation, is a good way to resolve the problems associated with foreign ownership of U.S. real estate. If a single piece of real property is the sole asset of a particular domestic corporation, it is even possible to sell the stock in the domestic corporation and thus transfer ownership of the asset without changing title.

For the best deals, or if foreign ownership of domestic real property is too much of a hassle, it may be best to look beyond the United States. Real estate values in Brussels will quadruple in the next five years. In 1992 Brussels, Belgium becomes the Washington, D.C. of a unified Europe. The EC/EU will represent 350 million people with a standard of living equal to ours. Many European banks are actively engaged in real estate finance. The Royal Trust Bank in

London has a department specifically designed to deal with foreign real estate investors. You can take advantage of this source of funds.

Buying Gold in Austria and Storing it in Switzerland

The Royal Bank of Canada in Austria (formally FoCoBank and later Royal Trust Bank) has long been the best line for the purchase of hard assets by the U.S. citizen. It is also very good for small European corporations. Hard assets, gold and silver, can be purchased on a 50% margin account and then stored in Switzerland in the duty-free zone. Your $50,000 corporate investment can now represent a $100,000 asset on your balance sheet. Additionally, as the price of gold rises, as it probably will do in the next few years, it will appreciate tax free.

Using the Corporation to Fund Your Retirement

Using a deferred compensation program in your domestic corporation, together with the use of split premium techniques in your foreign corporation, it is possible to fund your retirement plan largely tax-free. Your domestic corporation can purchase a life insurance policy on your life, paid for out of foreign profits, with the benefits paid to your family estate or trust. Or, if you wish, you could fund a fully paid retirement program by converting the cash value to a life annuity all of this with a minimum tax factor in the United States. There are life insurance agents in the United States who are aware of this beneficial interaction with foreign corporations. This is a regular service of most international business consultants.

One of the common ways to capitalize a foreign corporation is for the client to purchase from the newly formed corporation a private annuity. This annuity will be non-revocable, have no early payments, have a fixed rate of return and begin paying back in a certain number of years. Such an annuity can make it possible to move several hundreds of thousands of dollars into the foreign company for its investment capital. The foreign company is obligated to begin to return the capital and interest to the annuitant. You set the beginning of the pay out period, say 20 years.

Your Need for Personal Income Subject to Tax

It always puzzles me why some people would rather have the money than the benefits the money can buy. Money in the bank offers little pleasure. Many people die with a large estate that has no beneficiaries or with an estate that they always planned to enjoy someday. If it is possible to set up a foreign corporation and properly fund it, you will find that the corporate entities can take care of you as long as necessary.

Then, with a simple "letter of wishes," the corporate secretary can note that your heirs are allowed to step into your position and continue the corporate activity. A corporation never dies except by the will of the stockholders. It's simple, why not let the corporation take care of you? Don't take a big salary. It is taxed! Always take enough to cover your lifestyle. This is necessary to avoid the IRS "Means Test."

105

Beware of the IRS "Means Test"

The IRS "Means Test" is quite simply a test the IRS places on your apparent wealth. If you live in a $500,000 house and drive a Mercedes, and have not earned enough to pay taxes for years, they will simply assign a salary level that would have made it possible for you to acquire those assets (the means). They will then tax that salary and leave you to defend the tax. In many cases it is cheaper to pay the tax than to disclose your activities for the last 20 years.

We (LAD Financial Services) recommend to our international clients that they always take a small salary and, as happy U.S. citizens, pay the 15% or 25% tax on the amount subject to tax. You can always borrow money from a corporation. You must substantiate the loan, and pay it back at a fixed time. You can have some input into the interest rate to be paid, and it may be best to set it at a very high interest rate, subject to change. The properly filled-out loan document is in many cases sufficient evidence of your source of funds. However, you must be earning enough to show the ability to pay it back, so there is a bit of a catch-22.

Always remember, the object is to move money from the high-tax state to the low-tax state. Therefore, paying high interest rates to a financial institution is one of the best ways to do it. This is especially true if the interest is deductible. You might consider getting a home equity loan from a well-funded foreign corporation. You can then deduct the interest paid on your U.S. tax form.

Another benefit, that is often overlooked, is the ability of a foreign corporation to provide scholarships to worthy students anywhere in the world. Is it possible that your child could get a scholarship to Harvard or Brigham Young University from a foreign corporation where you had a position of influence? The process of planning and granting

106

scholarships is something that is handled completely by the board of directors of the corporation.

A student who accepts a scholarship provided by a foreign corporation should be sure that the grant is not structured in a way that he or she personally receives the funds. Such a transaction would result in the need to declare the income. If the corporation paid the funds directly to the school and then granted a scholarship to a worthy student, this would not be taxable. The corporation could select the "worthy student" to whom it wished to grant the scholarship. Or if the student chose to go to school abroad, there is no question that the transaction does not involve a relationship with the U.S. government.

Summary:
A World of Benefits Waits for You

In this section of "How and Why Americans Go Offshore," we have outlined many ways that you as an employee of a foreign corporation can receive many tangible benefits that can have an effect on your life-style. If you have read Charles Givens books or have heard lectures by speakers like Jack Miller, you are aware of the many deductible benefits that can be paid by a company in your behalf.

Simply transfer that mind set to the foreign company and realize that because it is not subject to tax at any level deductibility is not a matter of concern. Your only concern is how best to enjoy the benefits the company chooses to provide. It is our sincere desire that you will see the possibility in setting up such a structure for yourself and, with the help of a concerned and knowledgeable business and financial planner, begin to enjoy life as it was meant to be.

107

Notes:

12
Trusts and Asset Protection

A Word About Trusts

The first option to consider in asset protection is the use of a domestic trust with international options, or an international asset protection trust. Trusts have long existed as means for an individual to place their assets away from their immediate power and into the hands of a responsible representative for the benefit of a certain group of people, or beneficiaries.

The first trusts were created by monks who took a vow of poverty and didn't want to "own" the monastery. They chose to create an artificial person who would hold title to the asset, freeing them to declare poverty, and use that asset in a way that would benefit the order.

Modern society has built on this original canon law trust to create common law trusts, upon which most trust law still is built. A trust is simply an instrument that creates an artificial person to act on your granted assets in a way that will benefit your list of beneficiaries. A properly constituted trust must have three separate elements: grantor, trustee, and beneficiary. Without these three elements the entity is not a trust. If it does not fit these criteria, you may run into problems with the IRS, which may regard the trust simply as your alter ego.

Trusts are similar to corporations, with the important exception that a corporation allows you to work with the management to operate your business. Ideally, the proper trustee is totally independent of the grantor. The grantor may be appointed to an advisory committee to the trustee; however, the grantor should avoid absolute power of that committee. The grantor must remember that the advisory committee offers only non-binding advice, not binding direction.

Types of Trusts in Common Use Today

The most common domestic trust today is the *living trust*, so called because it is created while you are living to handle the affairs of your estate. The living trust is only good to avoid the costs of probate on the death of the first spouse. No one should have a will without at least taking advantage of the living trust.

The *Massachusetts business trust* is one of the best and oldest trust instruments in place and is still available to us. The trustee can be your foreign corporation. The Massachusetts business trust was very commonly used by the early business giants in the early stages of the industrial revolution. It was through the use of this trust that the Rockefeller's, Kennedy's, Melon's, and many others were able to accumulate the vast fortunes that sustain these families to this day.

The religious or tax-exempt trust is based on canon law and is commonly used by churches and religious foundations. There are some little-known religious orders that use trusts as a doctrine of faith. These trusts are religious instruments and protected by the First Amendment to the U.S. Constitution. Under this protection, these trusts are probably the only type that is exempt from the U.S. government's reporting requirement.

A trust based on canon law that has certain procedures institutionalized as sacraments can offer some very profound protections with regard to privacy and protection within the jurisdiction of the United States that are unattainable from any other source. We, at LAD Financial Services are aware of one such religious foundation trust that offers, within its church-based structure, the ability to have assets held in the corpus of the trust and moved offshore to a foreign jurisdiction though a collapsing bridge technique. These offshore trust itself can act as the holding company in the international structure and function as an operating foreign-based company that is not owned by the U.S. citizen, as outlined in the following chapters.

Utilizing Foreign Trust Structures

A very good method of pure asset protection is the combination of the "foreign situs asset protection trust" and the use of a "family limited partnership". The structure, as it is generally promoted, has the client who is the U. S. citizen as the general partner, owning 1% of the partnership. The foreign trust holds title to 99% of the partnership. This structure offers the client pure and complete asset protection. There is no tax advantage. For all tax purposes the trust is treated as a U.S. trust. It therefore is tax-neutral.

The safety is that in order to sue, any creditor or plaintiff's attorney would have to try the case in, for instance, the Isle of Man under Manx law. In that foreign jurisdiction the trust is only recognized, not the individual. This sets up a frustrating and insurmountable set of circumstances that offers complete protection. Indeed, the foreign asset protection trust opens a new area of privacy and asset protection.

International trusts, as those with which we are familiar domestically, allow an individual to grant or transfer assets to the discretionary power of a trustee. The trustee is responsible for management of assets in a way that will preserve and protect those assets on behalf of named beneficiaries. If it is a revocable trust, where the grantor has retained certain powers over the assets in trust such as the power to take those assets back into his or her control, the grantor must then continue to claim the value of these assets in their estate. The grantor is also required to file the trust tax forms and to pay the appropriate tax.

If for any reason the grantor elects to sever all connection with the trust administration, such as to resign as co-trustee or member of the trustee advisory committee, and at the same time elects to make the trust an irrevocable trust, thereby cutting off any claim to the assets held in trust, the grantor can effectively transfer title to these assets offshore permanently. If the trustee is a well-known trust bank such as Royal Bank of Canada, Barclays, or Royal Bank of Scotland, to name a few, the grantor can be assured that his or her assets are safe and that the trust will continue to be administered in a way that the grantor's named beneficiaries are protected and provided for well into the future. Additionally, because the grantor has resigned as co-trustee and elected to make the trust irrevocable, the responsibility of filing tax forms and paying taxes falls to the trustee. The trustee, depending on the jurisdiction, may or may not be required to file any tax forms.

If this trust is established in a jurisdiction where no tax is levied on trusts established by non-resident aliens, the grantor has effectively moved their assets into a jurisdiction where the trust's value can compound tax free over time.

When the beneficiaries take constructive receipt of the proceeds of the trust, or of the trust corpus, they will then need to claim the income and pay the appropriate tax on the money they receive.

In this era of litigation, the foreign asset protection trust is becoming very popular for almost any imaginary problem. It is an effective and useful tool to protect your assets against any predator. It can also hold the stock of your foreign corporation, or the interest you have in a Family Limited Partnership as an asset in trust.

The Importance of Jurisdiction

In dealing with trusts, as well as other entities, we should never forget the importance of jurisdiction. Any asset held offshore creates circumstances that are almost impossible to overcome by a creditor or plaintiff's lawyer in their effort to access your assets. Courts in tax haven jurisdictions will not recognize court orders from outside their jurisdiction. This creates an extra shield of protection for your assets. It is as if the asset protection trust creates a fortress but the simple act of domiciling it offshore creates a mote around the fortress.

Another aspect of trusts that should be clearly understood is the idea of revocable verses irrevocable. How freely you are able to regain power over the asset is essential to this difference. If it is possible for you to take the asset back into your power, you have a revocable trust. If you cannot, your trust is irrevocable. This is very important when it comes to reporting the existence of a trust as well as the assets held in trust.

It is the responsibility of the grantor to report the assets in a revocable trust. The grantor also must file the annual tax forms when applicable. In most cases a revocable trust is simply another way to hold your assets. However, in the case of an irrevocable trust, the picture changes drastically. This is especially true if the trust is a foreign asset protection trust.

It is the trustee who must report the assets in an irrevocable trust. The trustee also is responsible to report the gain in asset value and pay the tax, if this is required in his or her jurisdiction. So, if your trust is irrevocable and structured offshore, there is no way you can get the assets back, and therefore they cannot and need not be reported to the U.S. government. The trust is outside its jurisdiction.

From an operational standpoint, the trust can work similarly to the corporation, with the exception that the trustee is the operative person or entity. It is interesting that a foreign corporation can be a trustee or a co-trustee with a bank or trustee committee. Assets once granted or sold to a trust or corporation, and moved by title, are safe from any creditor with designs on your assets or your wealth. No court can gain access to information without cause. If you didn't own it, and did not fraudulently transfer it, they have no cause. Your assets are safe.

The Role of the Protector

Foreign asset protection trusts are irrevocable and all assets are put into the hands of the trustee for their discretionary use, with the express purpose that he or she is to administer the trust for the benefit and good of the beneficiaries. This opens up a clear dilemma. Inasmuch as the trustee is the guardian of your assets and you have no further power over them, you have the right to ask, "Who Guards the Guardian?" Mr. Martin Jennings, an international attorney from Spain, has written an article by that title on the proper role of a *protector*.

Trusts established now may be in existence in the second half of the next century. In the intervening period, it would be a fair assumption that there will be changes in politics, tax, trust law, and the suitability of particular trustees and the jurisdictions in which they administer their trusts. Once the trustee or trusts jurisdiction has been chosen, there is little room for complacency. Circumstances can change rapidly. It is in the interest of grantors and beneficiaries to ensure that the trust arrangements be able to adapt to changing circumstances and requirements.

I will quote from Mr. Martin Jennings Who Guards the Guardian article because the U.S. citizen who does not normally have contact with the protector in his or her trust arrangement. There may be questions that arise and need to be answered.

> "Protectors are most commonly used with discretionary trusts where frequently one of the main worries of the grantor and potential beneficiaries alike may be the lack of control over trustees and the absence of enforceable accountability," Mr. Jennings writes. "The protector is not an adversary to the trustee. He is someone who shares certain discretion and powers in a trust in which a clear emphasis is placed on the trustee function as a custodian. So it is that it has almost become a touchstone of integrity whether or not trustees welcome or discourage the use of a protector who can initiate change and enforce requisite accountability."

A protector acts in a role that falls short of that of the trustee. The protector is appointed to oversee various functions that are best not exercised exclusively by the trustee. For example, the protector may have powers to remove the trustee, fix or approve the trustee's remuneration, or move the trust to a more suitable jurisdiction. The protector should be appointed coincident with the establishment of the trust. It is best if this not be done as an afterthought. Provision for the appointment of the protector should be included in the trust document.

The answer to the question, "Who may be the protector?" is dependent largely on the powers conferred upon that person. It could be a trusted friend of the grantor, one who lives in another jurisdiction. But age, lack of expertise, and other factors may limit the ability of the grantor to find such a person. In answer to this problem, it is becoming more common to see separate independent corporate protectors who can be bonded and placed in a position to oversee the affairs of a given trust.

The powers of the protector may include the right to move the trust to a jurisdiction where the original intentions of the grantor are more consistently followed. In the event that there is a change in law in any given jurisdiction, it is incumbent upon the protector to review the situation and make such a change if it is indicated. The protector must have the power to make or authorize changes in the trust in the event jurisdictional law or the tax law is changed and affects the trust in its original intention. The protector must have the power to change trustees.

There may be any number of reasons in which it is undesirable that the existing trustees should continue to act. The protector, exercising his or her power of appointment of and dismissal of trustees, may change trustees. Through this express power, the protector will be able to bring about other changes, for it is always a sanction against a recalcitrant trustee that that individual may be removed.

Additionally, the protector has powers with regard to the appointment of auditors, and to review and require certain levels of fiduciary bonding of those entrusted with the management of the trust funds. The protector may also be involved in the appointment of investment managers. It is becoming increasingly common for grantors to recognize that trust functions can be broken down between organizations especially suited to perform particular roles. For instance, the ability to hold investment proceeds is quite distinct from the ability to manage them. The initial appointment of the investment manager is likely to be made by the grantor. Subsequently, this is perhaps best shared between the trustee and the protector.

As you can see, the role of a protector, though not common in U.S. trust law, is not only common but advisable in the case of use of a foreign asset protection trust. In those cases where we find that a trust protector is needed to add to the security of the entity on behalf of our clients, Intercon Associates provides a company protector. We, at Intercon Associates are then in a position to act as the original foreign grantor and as the protector through Papillon Limited. We have thus set up a structure that meets all of the qualifications of a foreign grantor trust as outlined by the IRS to meet the criteria for Revenue Ruling 69-70.

A Caveat About the Caymans

We, at Intercon Associates do not recommend or use the Cayman Islands for a general trust. There is provision in the Caymans for a special exempt trust. The use of the Cayman Islands as a jurisdiction for general trust formation is not the best because of the need to establish a bank as the underlying entity. The law concerning trusts in the Cayman Islands is complex in many of its aspects. Essentially, they recognize that a trust is a device whereby the legal and beneficial interests in an asset are held by separate persons. Usually a person (known as the settlor) transfers legal title to real or personal property to another (known as the trustee). There has been some recent work on the trust law in the Cayman Islands that might make this reservation mute. All tax haven jurisdictions are making every effort to clean up trust law to attract the considerable amount of trust business from jurisdictions like the United States. In all cases the trustee is obliged to deal with the property in accordance with the terms of the trust. The terms of the trust are usually set out in the trust deed or deed of settlement. The persons on whose behalf the property is held are known as beneficiaries.

Trusts may either be fixed, allowing the trustee no discretion as to which beneficiaries may benefit, or discretionary, in which case the trustee individually determines who among the class of beneficiaries is to receive the benefit of the trust property. The uses of trusts are manifold but the most common reasons for establishing a trust in the Cayman Islands would be to legally minimize the incidence of income tax; capital gains, transfer tax, or estate duties imposed in high tax areas; and to provide anonymity of ownership of the trust assets.

The Cayman Islands trust law provides for the creation of an exempted trust. The trust may obtain an undertaking from the government of the Cayman Islands. In such a case, the trust will not be subject to any taxation imposed in the islands, for a period of 50 years, from the date of its creation. Any company that provides trust services must first obtain a license under the Cayman Islands Banks and Trust Companies Regulation Law 1966, although individuals are not so required. In practice, the majority of trusts are administered by the commercial trust companies located in the islands. The requirement to first establish a bank in the Cayman Islands does not apply to the exempted trust.

Asset Protection
Through the Use of Trusts

In recent years, both business and professional people have become increasingly fearful of exposure to catastrophic financial loss resulting from a finding of liability for some form of alleged damages to a third party. The explosion in commercial litigation in the past 15 years has resulted in soaring insurance premiums, legal defense costs, and jury awards.

A little-noticed by-product of this trend is the gradual expansion of theories of liability adopted by the courts. This range from the recent judgments granted in the tobacco manufacturers' liability cases, to a professional liability action against clergymen in California, for failure to prevent teen suicide. The results oriented posture adopted by many courts has caused business and professional people to question whether the legal system has become a vehicle for the redistribution of wealth.

A state Supreme Court justice was recently quoted as saying, "As long as I am allowed to redistribute wealth from out-of-state companies to injured in-state plaintiffs, I shall continue to do so. Not only is my sleep enhanced when I give someone else's money away, but so is my job security, because in-state plaintiffs, their families and their friends will re-elect me."

In order to minimize their exposure to the risk of uninsured and unanticipated catastrophic loss resulting from an adverse judgment, many people have sought to minimize their risk through a number of estate-planning techniques.

119

We will briefly examine conventional techniques and contrast those with the use of a foreign asset protection trust.

The Ideal Asset Protection Structure

We believe that the best possible asset protection structure is in the combination of the use of a foreign situs asset protection trust; and the use of a Family Limited Partnership in the United States. Throughout "How and Why Americans Go Offshore" we have cited many examples of the use of these structures. They are both effective and legal and are recognized as such by the taxing authorities of each of the jurisdictions involved. The only improvement to this would be to use a foreign grantor trust or a foreign discretionary trust that would move the asset offshore and would add very effective tax benefits to the asset protection provision of the trust scheme.

The Foreign Non-Grantor Trust

This trust is the best possible foreign entity for tax, estate, and asset protection planning. It is the foreign discretionary trust and is irrevocable and out of the power of the grantor. This is the trust structure that is firmly and completely in the hands of the foreign trustee. Such a trust offers absolute protection from all predators of any kind.

The disadvantage of the inexperienced person is that he feels deprived of his asset since he does part with them completely. The experienced international person will recognize that under common law the trustee will respond to suggestions as if they were orders and will generally follow the consultants' suggestions without question. It is with this thought in mind that we, at Intercon Associates generally appoint the client to a position of managing consultant with specific responsibilities for the source and application of funds thus giving him some reason to offer suggestions in those areas where he is most concerned.

If the foreign situs asset protection trust proves to be expensive and as such is not well suited to the client's budget, we do not hesitate to recommend the anstalt, guarantee or hybrid company; as a suitable substitute in the scheme. If these are properly created and owned, there is equal protection from creditors and equal privacy from government agency inquiry. In order to clearly understand the process, it is important to review the traditional asset protection structures available to us today, as well as to look for ways to integrate what we know and understand with new programs available in the international financial marketplace.

Traditional Planning Techniques

Clients wishing to minimize the exposure of personal assets to the claims of business or professional creditors are generally advised to transfer ownership of such assets to spouses or other family members, either directly or in trust. Following such advice typically involves certain trade-offs that are often unpalatable to the client.

Outright Transfers

Outright transfers or direct transfers outside of trusts almost always are subject to federal gift tax. The impact of the gift tax may be minimized or eliminated with the use of the $10,000 annual exclusion, the unlimited marital deductions for inter spousal transfers, or the unified credit.

One should also consider the advisability of the immediate use the one time gift exemption of $600,000 per person that is allowed in your estate and is the basis for the A-B trust program. Clearly, if this is used now, in 1993, it is not available in the estate planning module, but with the real possibility of changes in the law effecting the limits of that allowance it might not be a bad idea to use it now while it is still at the high point.

The principal objection to outright gifts is loss of power. Transfer of ownership typically involves the surrender of all rights to the disposition and enjoyment of an asset, often to a spouse or family member inexperienced in its management. Lack of marital stability or otherwise unstable relationships can compound this problem. The use of the family limited partnership mitigates this problem in that the general partners, the parents, will always retain power as long as they are alive and will only gift to the children their limited partnership interests.

Transfers in Trust

Transfers in trust and gifts in trust may or may not be subject to the federal gift tax, depending upon the "strings" still attached to the grantor. For instance, the retention of a power of appointment or the right to alter, amend, or revoke the trust will result in an incomplete gift for federal gift tax purposes. Thus, not be subjected to taxation until trust distributions are made.

Unfortunately, retention of rights or powers over the enjoyment of trust property, while providing some relief from the feeling of loss of power, will frequently result in such property being included in the grantor's estate for purposes of creditor attachment. Courts have long held that the assets of a trust created by a grantor for his or her own benefit, even one containing spendthrift provisions, may be reached by creditors. A corollary rule is that assets of a discretionary trust may be reached by the grantor's creditors to the extent such assets may be applied for the benefit of the grantor.

Recent case law has extended the reach of creditors to the assets of trusts where the grantor has merely retained the power, as opposed to rights to enjoyment of trust property. For example, reservation of the right to amend or revoke, or to direct disposition of principal and income, has been held to subject trust assets to the claims to the grantor's creditors. Grantors seeking to place assets beyond the reach of their creditors by transfer to a domestic trust must therefore be prepared to sever all ties to such property.

Fraudulent Conveyance Issues

Though concerns about fraudulent transfer are important and are a major topic of discussion at all international asset protection conferences, we have yet to hear of a successful challenge to a transfer to trust or to a properly structured company that has been taken through the system to conclusion. Assuming the transferor is prepared to part with both power and enjoyment of his or her property, a transfer that is determined to intentionally "hinder, delay, or defraud" creditors will be voided as a fraudulent conveyance. Property so transferred will be judicially retitled in the name of the transferor and made subject to attachment by creditors. It should be clear, however, that liquid assets so transferred would most likely be lost in the system and not returnable.

The establishment of the transferor's intent is by its nature a subjective determination. Over the years, the courts have identified certain *badges of fraud* that are deemed to create the presumption that the transferor intended to hinder, delay, or defraud creditors, such as the following.:

- Insolvency of the transferor at the time of the transfer or as a result of the transfer.

- Transfers to family members or otherwise for inadequate consideration.

- Secrecy or concealment of the conveyance.

- Transfers made while litigation is pending or threatened.

- The retention of any power or enjoyment of assets.

The demonstration of the existence of one or more of such badges shifts the burden of proof to the transferor in order to rebut the presumption that the transfer was made with fraudulent intent.

Proof of negative facts is often extremely difficult, thus forcing the transferor to establish evidence of intent to accomplish bona fide goals as the result of the transfer. Which creditors are entitled to claim they were defrauded, and the burden of proof required to establish such fraud, depends upon the status of each creditor's claim at the time of the transfer. The physician who quitclaims title to real estate in favor of his or her spouse the day after suffering a malpractice judgment clearly has a lot of explaining to do. Likewise the physician who has been served with a complaint seeking malpractice damages in excess of the limits of the doctor's insurance coverage.

On the other hand, the physician who merely fears that someday he or she may be forced to defend such action as a risk of practicing medicine is free to make such a transfer. At least one court has held, in the absence of identifiable creditors, "the right of the (transferor) to dispose of his property as he saw proper, was absolute and unconditioned. His intent in doing so was wholly immaterial...where there is no creditor, there is no fraud, and therefore no policy of the law to prevent the enforcement of the trust...." Crucial differences result from the legal distinctions made among present, future, and potential creditors.

Present creditors are generally those creditors who have matured claims against the transferor, such as judgment creditors who have prevailed in litigation against the transferor, or mortgage lenders who have foreclosed against real estate collateral and have established a deficiency under applicable state law. Future creditors are presently identifiable parties whose currently inchoate claims may foreseeably ripen into rights enforceable against the transferor's property, such as plaintiffs in pending litigation or mortgagees of half-empty office buildings. Potential creditors are those currently unidentifiable claimants who haunt the dreams of obstetricians, directors of public companies, and business people who suffer free-floating anxiety about the possibility of becoming targets of predatory litigation.

The defense of a fraudulent conveyance claim brought by a present creditor is the most challenging under the Uniform Fraudulent Conveyance Act, adopted in 16 states, and the Uniform Fraudulent Transfer Act, adopted in 17 states. In contrast, a successful fraudulent conveyance claim brought by a future creditor requires proof of actual intent to defraud. Potential creditors cannot avail themselves of such a claim because, as one court has said, "...motives with

125

which such a conveyance is made and the fears by which it is prompted are of no importance...." Thus, transfers that are prompted by the fear of identifiable creditors, present or future, are likely to be overturned. Transfers made out of fear that a present or future creditor might emerge are not tainted. Accordingly, asset protection planning should be viewed as a vaccine, not as a cure.

Having clearly stated the above with regard to the letter of the law, I must say that in the many years that I have been involved with international trusts, I have never heard of a successful prosecution of a case of fraudulent transfer in a foreign (business haven) jurisdiction. This is true even in the cases where it is obvious such as transfers made after the fact of a judgment against the transferor.

Advantages of a Foreign Situs Trust

The principal disadvantages of conventional asset protection techniques are loss of both power and control. Both can be substantially retained through the use of an artfully crafted foreign trust or domestic limited partnership structure.

The Trust

Although the creditors of a grantor of a domestic trust can reach the trust corpus where the grantor has retained rights that might lead to his or her enjoyment of trust assets, this principle does not extend categorically to the laws of other democracies. There are several common law jurisdictions that neither grant similar rights to creditors nor recognizes the judgments of the courts of those jurisdictions that do grant such rights.

There is no legal bar to a citizen or resident of the United States settling a trust under the more favorable laws of a foreign jurisdiction, provided there are adequate contacts with such jurisdiction to justify such choice of law. This principle is analogous to that allowing the choice of Nevada law for the organization and governance of a corporation, despite the location of its principal offices and management personnel in another state.

The choice of New York law has similarly been upheld in a will contest against the estate of decedent domiciled in France who executed a will there to dispose of property located in that country. She chose New York law as a planning technique to avoid the French "forced heirship" law that would have awarded half of her estate to her son.

Depending upon the laws of the jurisdiction governing the settlement of the trust, the level of both enjoyment and control that may be vested in the grantor may represent a significant enhancement over the rights and powers that may be retained by grantors of domestic trusts. Properly drafted, a foreign situs trust may result in little or no diminution of such attributes.

The Limited Partnership

The common objection voiced by clients to whom settlement of an inter vivos or "living" trust, domestic or foreign, is recommended is that the appointment of third party trustees would rob them of the autonomy and the power that accompany outright ownership. This concern can he assuaged by the use of a limited partnership as a subsidiary of the trust, with the client as general partner.

All property to be protected can first be conveyed to the partnership by the client, 1% as a general partner and 99% as a limited partner (with a second party contributing a nominal amount to qualify as the necessary second partner of the partnership).

The 99% limited partner interest can then be immediately transferred to the foreign situs trust, beyond the reach of potential creditors. The client reserves 100% power over the assets of the partnership while retaining only a 1% interest therein as general partner.

A collateral benefit of the use of a limited partnership is the limited remedy available to creditors or the transferor. Assuming that a creditor is successful in challenging a transfer, on fraudulent conveyance grounds, the creditor is entitled to no monetary damages. Rather, the remedy is an equitable one, i.e., the court orders the unwinding of the transfer(s) that rendered the transferor insolvent.

In the sequence set forth above, the transfer to the limited partnership does not render the client insolvent, since he or she receives partnership interests with a value that is equivalent to that of the properties he or she conveyed to the partnership. If any transfer can be argued to have rendered the client insolvent, it is the subsequent transfer of his or her 99% limited partnership interest to the trust. A judicial reversal of the transaction that rendered the debtor insolvent would retitle the transferred limited partnership interest in the name of the transferor-limited partner, thus giving his or her creditors the opportunity to pursue all of the remedies available to the creditors or limited partners.

Under the Revised Uniform Limited Partnership Act, the sole remedy available to such creditors is a *charging order*, entitling the creditor to receive whatever distributions of partnership income or capital that would have otherwise been made to the debtor. The creditor does not become a substitute limited partner and therefore does not succeed to have power over the voting or other rights (such as authority to remove the general partner) that limited partners customarily enjoy. Rather, the creditor is placed in the passive role of "assignee" of the debtor's interest.

This remedy is a double-edged sword, in light of the IRS ruling that such assignees are taxable on their debtors' pro rata shares or partnership income and gain, regardless of whether or not accompanying distributions are made. Thus, it is not inconceivable that the debtor, as general partner, would be in a position to manage partnership affairs in such a manner as to deprive creditors of cash distributions, while causing them to recognize taxable income. The debtor's bargaining position is drastically improved.

Tax Consequences

The foreign situs trust or domestic limited partnership structure is essentially tax-neutral in that it does not materially alter the federal income, estate, or gift tax situation of most clients. For income tax purposes, 99% of all partnership items flow through the trust to the client's personal income tax return, since the trust is treated as a "grantor" trust.

Transfers can be made free of federal gift tax. This is achieved by the retention of a limited power of appointment by the trust settlor. This gives the settlor a certain flexibility and renders the transfer an incomplete gift for gift tax purposes. Because of the retained powers of the settlor, trust assets are includible in their estate for federal estate tax purposes.

The Internal Revenue Code imposes an excise tax on the transfer of appreciated property to foreign trusts and other entities. The tax is imposed on the excess or the fair market value of property transferred over its adjusted basis in the hands of the transferor. Although the line of demarcation between domestic and foreign trusts is relatively unclear, careful draftsmanship should yield a trust that qualifies as a U.S. trust for federal tax purposes while being deemed a foreign trust for all other purposes. A safety net is provided by an IRS ruling holding the excise tax inapplicable as long as the trust is treated as a grantor trust for federal income tax purposes.

The goal of asset protection and asset power and enjoyment need not be mutually exclusive. Opening one's mind to the advantages offered by compatible foreign legal systems can allow the achievement of these twin goals.

13
Captive Insurance

Captive Insurance Companies in Asset Protection

A Preview of Captive Insurance

The use of captive insurance companies is an excellent mean of protection of assets and accumulation of tax-deferred income toward a retirement account. The best jurisdictions are the Cayman Islands and in the Isle of Man, which have designed their business laws to deal effectively with the captive insurance needs of our clients.

The growth of the captive insurance industry is directly related to the ease of obtaining large settlements and judgments in U.S. courts. Multi-million dollar judgments are common and the protection that is offered to the client who is part of a captive group is outstanding.

A captive insurance company is a company that is owned by or sells its product to a certain affinity group, as opposed to the public offering of insurance products. We use doctors as an example because health care is the profession with which I am most conversant. The rules, however, apply to any group that may be experiencing rises in their insurance costs.

With the uncontrolled rise in insurance costs many groups of doctors, as well as other affinity groups, are finding that owning their own insurance company offers an excellent investment opportunity, as well as adequate insurance against the occasional legitimate claim.

A captive insurance company can be owned by individual stockholders or by a foreign corporation. In either case, the objective and modus operandi is the same. It is a function of any insurance company to set aside a certain amount of money for payment of claims. The balance is invested on behalf of the company and its stockholders.

The doctors' captive insurance company continues to charge high (market rate) premiums to their stateside operations. These premiums are paid to a company controlled by the group, and all excess premiums are invested in a way that builds retirement benefits for the individual member.

In this case, the doctors' liability is reinsured with a reputable company such as Lloyds of London, and the balance of the premium is available for investment. The investment committee, generally made up of members of the group, meets and decides the specific investments for the company.

The investment committee may choose to invest in the office building where the medical group practices, or other assets that previously were directly controlled by the individual doctor. In this case, assets are moved from personal power to the insurance company's power, out of reach of any creditor.

As you can see, this is an alternative to protection of one's assets. Protection, in light of the malpractice liability problem that presents itself to the professional person. These offshore opportunities are also available to the manufacturer who is dealing with a product or service that is vulnerable to excessive product liability.

An international business or financial consultant who has a working knowledge in the area of international business structure can be an important member of your financial advisory team.

A captive insurance company is a company owned by or selling its product to a certain affinity group, as opposed to the public offering of insurance products. Its members can include its parent company as well as members of almost any professional group.

The use of captive insurance companies is most commonly looked at in today's litigious society by doctors. Doctors, who have been in the forefront in the need for asset protection from malicious lawsuits. Now, many other affinity groups are finding that they, too, can benefit from a wholly owned captive insurance company.

Lately in a turn of poetic justice, attorneys are finding themselves on the defendant end of malpractice suits. Perhaps they will be the next group to find that captive insurance is the best way to go.

Laws in jurisdictions like the Cayman Islands, the Isle of Man, and the Channel Islands are ideal for the formation and operation of captive insurance companies. There is considerable information available with regard to these rules illustrative of what is available. A summary of those related to the Cayman Islands is contained in Appendix II "The Cayman Islands."

It is now generally accepted that the offshore captive insurance industry represents an important sector of the international insurance market. With more than 350 licensed offshore insurers, the Cayman Islands are acknowledged as being one of the major offshore insurance centers.

The licensed companies include the traditional parent only captive, more mature captives assuming unrelated treaty reinsurance business, association or industry captives, and privately owned insurance and reinsurance companies.

Classes of business covered are widespread, the most common coverage being workers' compensation, comprehensive, general and property liability, medical malpractice, products liability, and all classes of life assurance.

Reasons for Development

The Cayman Islands first experienced significant growth in offshore insurance business in the mid-1970s. The principal reasons for this have been the following.

- An existing reputation as a stable tax shelter and center for international banking.

- A sound professional infrastructure that had already developed to serve these industries.

- Proximity to the United States.

- The introduction of the Cayman Islands' Insurance Law 1979.

The Cayman Islands' Insurance Law 1979 and Regulations

The Cayman Islands' government had two basic objectives in introducing the insurance law. First, it introduced regulations to cover the operations of domestic insurers, with the primary objective of protecting the interests of local policyholders. Second, it was designed to encourage the development of offshore insurance business, at the same time ensuring that the Islands' reputation as an offshore financial center would not be brought into disrepute by any dubious insurance business.

The law therefore introduced licensing requirements for all insurers, brokers, agents and underwriting managers. With respect to insurers, there are two principal license categories: the Class-A license for domestic insurers, and the Class-B license, either restricted or unrestricted, for offshore companies. The concept of the restricted license was intended for the parent-only captive situation and such licensees must give an undertaking to insure or reinsure risks of these shareholders only. However, almost 80 percent (80%) of Class-B licenses issued are unrestricted.

The supporting regulations provide the framework for licensing procedures and annual reporting requirements, also establishing the position of the Superintendent of Insurance. The Superintendent of Insurance is charged with the responsibility of reviewing and processing all applications and supervising compliance with annual reporting requirements.

Information to be included in the license application includes incorporation documents, details of all shareholders, directors and officers, underwriting managers, and auditors, and a business plan detailing the proposed business of the company. Net worth requirements must be met by unrestricted license holders, being $120,000 (U.S. dollars) for general business, $240,000 (U.S. dollars) for long-term business, and $360,000 (U.S. dollars) for a combination of both.

Annual reporting requirements include the preparation of audited financial statements in accordance with generally accepted accounting principles and a certificate of compliance to confirm that a company's operations have been in accordance with its business plan.

See Appendix II "The Cayman Islands" for a more extensive exploration of structures in the Cayman Islands. Further details concerning license application information, other licensing requirements, and incorporation and annual costs are set out in the booklets available from the "big eight" accounting firms in your chosen jurisdiction.

The Creative Use of Captive Insurance

Intercon Associates, through its association with several highly qualified individuals in Europe and the Cayman Islands, has created the model for a unique captive insurance program.

This captive insurance program brings together the best of the insurance concept with that of asset protection and estate planning. To understand and use the concept of the Intercon Associates system of the creative use of offshore captive insurance to its maximum benefit, it is necessary to discuss each of the players in a proper offshore scheme. Then we can show an integration of those players into a beneficial system for the client.

To that end, we will first look at the need for and creation of asset protection schemes that are essential to the financial well being of professionals in the United States today. Second, we will move on to look at the concept of captive Insurance. Third, we will look at a specific example of the Intercon Associate use of captives through the international indemnity insurance company. Finally, we will show how the proper and creative integration of the use of all three of these systems and concepts can result in not only insurance protection and asset protection, but a very interesting and beneficial relationship. All together this will create a sizable foreign based investment company that can be used in many beneficial ways for both the client and his family for years to come.

The Need for Insurance Protection

Who Needs It!

Every practicing doctor in the U.S. lives and works in fear that someday soon he will be charged with an act of malpractice and be subject to a lawsuit. This in many cases is true regardless of the quality of care he offers his patients or the amount of continuing education he provides for himself and his staff.

It is an undisputed fact of life that many people react instinctively to the inevitable accident or untoward result and claim malpractice. This has lead to a defensive mentality that directly impacts on the care we are given and more importantly the costs we are asked to bear. Many doctors will readily admit that much of the cost they pass on to the patient is in treatment or tests that will build a case for them should they ever be subject to a suit.

There was once a day when the idea of malpractice insurance was something that only doctors considered essential. Today the idea that we are all subject to devastating lawsuits has spread to virtually every profession and to most other business activities as well. One doctor said when he noticed in the paper that a lawyer was being sued for malpractice, "Though I hate to say it, there is such a thing as justice being done."

The United States has 70 percent of the world's lawyers. What with that large group of people looking for work you can always be sure that virtually every one of us is subject to a lawsuit at least once in our lifetime. Every year, one in four U.S. adults is sued. That is unless we talk about Washington, D.C., where the rate is one in every two.

This appears to be the result of two factors. First the widely held belief by members of our society that it is easier to acquire wealth by taking it from those who have it than by working for it. Second, the massive legal industry cited above that caters to that belief. Today your risks of being sued is proportional to what you own, **not** what you do.

Some Examples of Legal Greed

1. A driver was being chased by a Florida highway patrolman on a Miami street, reaching speeds of 85 m.p.h. His car crossed over the center divide and crashed into a large rock that Miami citizens fondly named Prudential. The driver was killed. Autopsy showed the blood level to be 0.26, well above the point of legal intoxication. Nevertheless, the widow sued the city for placing the rock in the center divide. She won a $2,000,000 judgment. The City of Miami was forced to assess residents additional taxes to get the money to pay the judgment.

2. A man, intent on burglarizing a West Coast school, was creeping across the school rooftop. He fell through the skylight and injured himself. He filed a suit against the school district and collected $260,000 cash, plus $1,200 a month for the rest of his life with a 3% cost of living increase. This turned out to be a much more successful robbery than he ever dreamed of initially.

3. A man attempted to commit suicide by jumping in front of a New York City subway train. The subway engineer saw him in time to stop the train and save the man's life. The man filed suit against the New York transit authority, the agency that operates the subways. The claim was for "intentional interference with a suicide attempt." He collects $600,000 cash.

4. A group of five unincorporated doctors operating as a general partnership sent their receptionist out to buy hot dogs for lunch. In her uninsured automobile she hit a university jogger and bruised his leg. The lawyer goes to the deepest pockets and sued the doctors. This was possible because the employee was in the course of her employment, for the benefit of the doctors. The Supreme Court affirmed a combined judgment against the doctors for $1.2 million.

There are cases where suits have been against third parties for taxes raised against family members. There are cases where property owners have been sued for damages that happened on property they no longer own. There are numerous cases of suits being filed for health problems arising out of the disposal of hazardous waste on property. Sometimes the current owner can not meet the cost of the judgment. In these cases the former owners are brought into the suit.

We could go on and on. The hunger of attorneys and the attitude of individuals in our society has combined to create a climate of constant and reasonable fear that each of us will someday be the object of a lawsuit. Insurance protection and offshore asset protection are the only alternatives. Fortunately, through the use of captive insurance companies, we have some control of the cost and some interest in the future of the industry.

The Doctor is Vulnerable,
But He is Not Alone

As stated earlier, the doctors' vulnerability to malpractice action is well documented and is a given matter of fact. It is a rare professional that can go through any reasonable lifetime of practice without at least one or two malpractice actions being brought against him. This is true regardless of the amount of care or quality of his practice technique.

There are many documented cases where a doctor's assets have been seized by plaintiff's attorneys and or governmental agencies, like the IRS. These are all in an effort to collect judgments that have been rendered against him or her. There is no question, that in the mind of many non-professional people, doctors are the top money makers in the country. Trying to figure out a way to transfer some of that money from the doctor to the plaintiff is in some circles nearly a sport.

It is a fact that the only people who get sued are those with money or with insurance. The first question that the plaintiff's attorney asks is, "Does he have insurance or what are his assets?" Such an attitude has created a new industry in America today. This is the field of asset protection.

There are many speakers who travel around the country offering doctors seminars on ways to protect their assets. It presents a formidable challenge. In most cases, structures can be created that will make it more difficult for the plaintiff's attorney to determine the amount of and to create ways to get access to those assets.

As stated earlier, one of the most common tools is a family limited partnership. The effect of the use of this tool is that the plaintiff may win the case and may be able to file a lien against the partnership, but his reward is limited to a *charging order* that delays any possibility of him seeing any real money until the general partner votes a distribution.

In the interim he is given a charging order that is filed against the partnership and is treated by the government as phantom income to the holder of the order. The plaintiff is then subject to tax on money he may never see. A plaintiff's attorney that files such an order on behalf of his client should be sued for malpractice himself. Since the act itself is so self defeating.

* Protection in Divorce

    Professional people, as well as most other members of society, are faced today with a growing divorce rate. Assets that have been accumulated by the family are now subject to a wrenching battle to divide and to separate so that each of the partners can get what he or she perceives to be its fair share.

Divorce attorneys are particularly adept at gaining some access to assets that might have been less visible to the general public. These assets become fair game in the divorce battle. Sometimes the effort for privacy in one's affairs creates a dichotomy. One must choose the route of letting everyone know what assets the household owns or giving up an unfair share to the divorcing spouse.

- The Safety of Your Pension Plan

  In the past one always thought that his pension plan was sacred and that plaintiff attorneys could not gain access to this asset. In recent years this is proving untrue. More and more often your pension plan assets are included in your general assets and are subject to any judgment. With that in mind it is essential that every professional person consider an alternative to the usual and customary way of protecting your assets and providing for your own personal care and comfort in your old age. Each of us must look out for ourselves and create ways to protect these assets from any predator.

The Intercon Concept of Captive Insurance

Simply defined, a captive insurance company is a corporation organized primarily to provide insurance for its owners or an affinity group of insured clients. This is accomplished by assuming all or part of its owner's exposure to financial loss as either direct insurance or reinsurance. A captive may have either one single parent stockholder, (pure captive) or many unrelated stockholders, (association captive). In both situations the captive provides initial insurance or reinsurance for its owners.

The captive concept has been in existence for many years. Current estimates indicate approximately 2000 captives exist worldwide. The vast majority of these captives being organized primarily to provide insurance or reinsurance for U.S. parent organizations, U.S. associations or U.S. professional organizations.

Several major insurance companies in the United States were originally captives. The Allstate Insurance

Company was once a captive, originally organized to provide insurance for its parent, Sears. The Belefonte Insurance Company was formed years ago to provide insurance for its parent Armco Steel. The list goes on and on.

When a captive begins to provide insurance or reinsurance for non-owners, the captive becomes a senior or profit center type captive. The first major growth period for the formation of new captives began in 1965 following Hurricane Betsy insurance companies began forcing major corporations to assume higher and higher property deductions following the disaster. Many responded by forming captives as a vehicle to fund these higher deductions.

During the mid 1970's the U.S. insurance industry suffered its worst underwriting results for casualty business in its history. We can only imagine the exposure the insurance industry will have after the 1992 season with hurricanes in Florida and Hawaii, the Southern California Coastal fires of 1993 and the devastating 1994 Los Angeles earthquake. Once again the business and professional community will turn to captives as a way to control what will become an explosion in premium costs.

The insurance industry always responds to exposure such as this with increased premium costs. Many businesses and professionals who would not have experienced adverse losses are forced to pay higher premiums to help off set the disastrous underwriting results of others. In addition, many insurance buyers were or will be unable to find coverage at any price.

Thus during the mid and late 1970's and most probably again following the disastrous year we have just witnessed a new wave of captive insurance formation took place. During the period following the 1970's approximately 600-700 new captives were formed to provide various coverage's for their parents.

Included in this new group of companies were those providing other coverage as well, such as medical malpractice, products liability, and professional liability. Current estimates indicate that the captive insurance industry underwrites between eight and ten billion dollars in annual premium volume.

During the late 1970's the U.S. insurance industry began to recoup its underwriting losses of the mid 1970's. The result was a return to competitive premium levels throughout the industry. However, at that point the captive concept had become well known and respected as a viable insurance alternative because of the inherent advantages and the formation of new captives has continued to grow.

The Current Market

This unfortunately was the case and now many insurance buyers who took the traditional approach are being forced to deal with drastic premium increases and restricted or no coverage. One of the major advantages of a captive insurance company is that of being a stable market from which the owners can purchase their insurance on a consistent basis. A captive would only have to increase its own premium levels to the extent it suffered poor underwriting results based on its own loss record and not that of others.

Other Advantages of the Captive

Another major advantage of the captive concept is increased cash flow and investment income implications. The captive, depending on its willingness to accept risk, and its accesses to the international market, retains the majority of the gross premium expenditures of the parent and invest this excess premium to gain a greater return. The captive can invest these funds and generate substantial profits through investment income.

In the casualty insurance business it takes between six and ten years to ultimately pay out or settle all losses incurred during a given policy year. The captive has use of these funds, during this period, in the form of loss reserves and is free to invest and generate additional investment income. The result is that when the captive generates these additional profits, it has the ability to reduce future premium levels or devise a way to directly or indirectly allocate that excess premium or profit share to the owners or members of the affinity group.

Other advantages include direct access to the reinsurance market. Since reinsurance companies traditionally assume a portion of the original risks undertaken by a primary insurance company, usually in the form of excess or catastrophic reinsurance, this market is not available to the insurance buying public. Through the use of a captive an insurance buyer can deal directly with the reinsurance market to secure necessary reinsurance protections to insure the long term success of the captive.

A simplistic example would be one where the captive would like to provide a $1,000,000 policy limit to its owners; but, due to the limited resources of the captive a $1,000,000 loss would be disastrous. The captive would go to the reinsurance market and "lay off" a large portion of the original policy limit. The captive may decide to retain the first $100,000 of loss and ask the reinsurance company to assume the next $900,000 of loss under the one million dollar policy limit.

In this example the captive has limited its maximum exposure in any one single loss to $100,000. The cost to the captive of this excess reinsurance may be only twenty-five to thirty percent of the captives original premium depending on the reinsurance underwriter's quotation. Thus the captive can assume only ten percent of the ultimate loss but retain between seventy and seventy-five percent of the original premium.

Another form of reinsurance called "aggregate stop loss." The aggregate stop loss would allow the captive to limit its total losses to a fixed amount, thus protecting the captive's financial integrity. Currently this type of reinsurance is hard to find and as a result requires either sizable capital contributions or assessment liabilities on the part of the captive members.

The final advantage we will cite here is that of the ability of the captive to improve insurance coverage for the members. While many traditional insurance underwriters often exclude certain exposures from the coverage, a captive is in a position of providing whatever coverage it deems appropriate to fulfill the needs of the members. This would mean that a captive could offer an insurance policy to cover excess automobile and contingent liability; in addition to the usual policy for protection against professional liability or casualty losses.

A Different Kind of Company
with a Multiple Purpose

The International Indemnity Insurance Company is a Cayman Islands company authorized to do business as an insurance company. It is chartered in the Cayman Islands and is administered by one of the most competent and qualified island insurance administrators available.

Its function is to provide a platform upon which certain groups of individuals, under the influence and power of various investment advisors or business advisors world wide can direct their interested clients. Each group has its own sub category and is subject to the underwriting requirements of the company underwriting committee. In this sense it is the embodiment of the *rent-a-captive* concept.

This would mean that a group of qualified and interested doctors or any other group of vulnerable individuals could form one subgroup and another could be a group of lawyers, body building gym operators or contractors. In each case the insurance carrier could cover the liability and the general insurance needs of the client.

How It Differs from the Standard Captive

As stated earlier, the premise under which a captive insurance company is formed is that the company exists to offer self insurance to the parent company. In this case there are some critical differences. The primary difference of this company from the standard captive is that the ownership or stockholders of the company are made up of people who are not the policy holders but companies the policy holders designate to represent their best interest.

147

That is to say that the stockholders of this company would be a group of Isle of Man or Gibraltar companies or trusts that hold stock in this insurance company as one of its investments. These companies would be formed on behalf of certain high net worth individuals who wish to take advantage of the offshore options that are available to United States citizens as outlined in this book.

So, the stock in this company would be held by a group of companies that are under the administration and power of Intercon Associates, Ltd. Then each Isle of Man company would appoint an individual, most probably the client who holds the position as managing consultant, to represent them at the annual meeting of stockholders where the board of directors and standing committees are annually re-appointed.

The Three Standing Committees

The insurance company would have three standing committees made up of members appointed by the officers of the company and entrusted with specific responsibility. The first and probably the most important would be the Underwriting Committee.

1. The Underwriting Committee

    The primary function of the underwriting committee is to evaluate the potential policy holder and to determine first, if he or she is a suitable client for the company and second, the level of premium that would be charged for the coverage provided. The spokesperson on behalf of the proposed insured would be the domestic business consultant who had submitted his name for insurance.

The committee would first approve the insured risk and then would set the premium level for the insured within the group from which he made his application. One should bear in mind that there are two levels of acceptance that each applicant must pass in order to be considered for coverage. First is the acceptance into the group that is sponsoring the applicant. Second is the risk as determined by the underwriting committee.

In its function as claims adjuster, the Underwriter Committee will recommend to the management certain guidelines that will be followed with regard to the payment or settlement of claims. It will be our recommended policy that all claims shall be tried and none settled without a fight. This will require that the claimant come to the Cayman Islands and file a claim in the courts of the Islands. Such a policy would deter a lot of mischievous unwarranted claims from being filed.

2. The Investment Committee

This is the second of the standing committees of the company. The responsibility of this committee will be to invest the reserves of the company in such a way as to generate the best possible return. The investment committee is made up of qualified investment advisors and would be expected to work for the best interest of the company.

The income generated by the investment committee is allocated to the general fund of the company and goes toward covering the costs with regard to management and administration. Excess income generated by this committee above and beyond the amount necessary to meet the projected return to the companies designated as recipients of any rebate would be distributed to the stockholder companies as dividends.

3. The Management Committee

The management committee is drawn from the stock-holders' representatives that would be appointed to the board of directors. This would be the group of individuals that would be in a position to go to the Cayman Islands and meet quarterly with the designated island manager and to offer direction and administrative assistance to the overall management of the company activities.

The management committee like the other two is annually reappointed. The management committee is in a position to act on behalf of the best interest of the company, the policy holders and the stockholders. It should be clear that this committee would be the group that establishes the agreement to accept additional groups into the company structure and the compensation the marketing agent for each group should be paid. That is to say as each domestic business or trust advisor puts together first an affinity group of interested potential policy holders, the board of directors would negotiate with the advisor for his role in the company and the compensation that role would carry.

The primary income to the marketing agent is the fee that is charged by the domestic affinity group for access to the insurance company as a benefit as outlined below. In as much as each group is self administered it is totally within the power of the domestic advisor that creates such a group of potential policy holders to set the fee for his income and to administer the affairs of the group as well.

The company is prepared to set a certain percentage of the paid in premium to be assigned to the sales and marketing effort. This would be based on what is normal for the industry and would be paid to the marketing agent or to a company designated by him as the recipient of any funds that otherwise would be paid in his behalf.

Sales in the United States

In order to make this insurance opportunity available within the United States without running up against the laws against solicitation, the marketing of this opportunity would take place as a benefit offered to members of an affinity group. That is each individual interested in taking advantage of this offer must first join a select group, or be a client of a business or insurance consultant who offers this opportunity as a service to his clients.

Each applicant for insurance to International Indemnity Insurance Company would be issued one share of common stock in the company. Thus, as a stockholder the applicant would be eligible for insurance in the captive. Some may choose to apply as members of a medical group or hospital staff that offers this coverage to its members. This would create a true affinity group under the normal definition of the term. Each member of the group or association should pay annual dues to belong and should expect to share in the benefits of membership including but not limited to the possibility of group offshore captive insurance coverage.

The set up and operation of this organization is of no concern of the insurance company. The organizer would seek participation in the insurance company for his members as a benefit of his organization. Each domestic business or marketing agent so inclined could set up and administer his own specific affinity group for clients of his who would be interested in access to such coverage.

An integral part of the application process would be the attachment of an application check that would pay for one share of common stock in the insurance company with all the benefits offered to common stock holders. The company would then contract with Intercon Associates to organize an offshore foreign company that could own additional shares in the insurance company.

The Role of the Stockholders

It should be noted at this point that with the exception of the single share of stock issued to each policyholder, virtually all of the stock of this insurance company would be held as investments of certain companies or trusts organized in some proper offshore jurisdiction. The appointed representative of these companies or trusts (the client) would serve on the board of directors, or on the committees of the insurance company.

The Preferred Stockholders

The company would issue two types of stock. Preferred stock would go to the founders of the company and the initial board of directors who would be entrusted with ongoing responsibility of company operations. Additional preferred stock might be made available to marketing representatives or to companies whose represent- ative served with honor as long time standing committee chairmen in recognition of service offered to the company.

The board of directors is drawn from the members of the company that are listed as preferred stockholders. It is assumed that these people would be most interested in the successful operations of the insurance company and would be actively involved in its management and growth.

The Common Stockholders

A single share of common stock would be issued to each policyholder with the proper application and payment of fees. This is to create the proper relationship to the captive insurance company. Additional shares of common stock could be issued to each offshore company in return for its investment in the company. In this case its managing consultant is also a policy holder with the insurance company.

The managing consultants will have joined the various affinity groups around the country that offer this type of insurance to its members as organized and promoted by the marketing staff. This would mean from a practical operational standpoint each individual seeking coverage through this hybrid captive would first become a stockholder, coincidental with that activity an Isle of Man company would be created for his use and the client would be appointed managing consultant to that company.

The payment of the fee to Intercon Associates to organize that company could come directly from the insurance company. Additionally, all ordinary costs of maintenance would be paid by the insurance company as a part of annual premium.

Upon approval of the insured by the underwriting committee the company so formed would receive shares in the insurance company as an investment. The company would appoint the insured to represent its interest on the list of stockholders of the insurance company thus would protect its interest in its investment.

The Role of Management

Management of the insurance company would be entrusted to the board of directors or to a management company who would be appointed by the stockholders at the annual meeting or by proxies obtained by the board at the time of the annual meeting. This would follow the usual and customary company operations procedure.

In the proforma models that have been generated for the operations of the insurance company allow for the following distribution of gross income. Ten percent (10%) of the paid in premium will be allocated to operating costs. Twenty percent (20%) of the paid in premium would be allocated to an account designated *permanent reserve*. This account is set aside to insure that the company will always be able to meet any claims in the low end risk area. Our administration of this account would be effected by prudent management and investment policy.

The generally accepted cost for reinsurance of the high end risk is 20% to 25% of the paid in premium. We, at International Indemnity insurance company would seek our reinsurance from such world renowned firms as Lloyds of London or Prudential.

Each year at the annual meeting the board of directors would declare a dividend to the stockholders and at the same time will establish a prudent reserve for the coming year based on the exposure and the amount of renewal premium funds on hand. In this sense the captive act as a mutual company owned by many independent entities that will share in the results of good management.

Advantages for the Insured

With regard to his insurance company, the insured professional would act no differently than he has in the past. He would pay his premium as determined by the underwriter and would be issued a certificate of insurance that would attest to the fact that he carried adequate insurance to satisfy those who require it.

In the event of a claim against him, he would notify the company of the claim and would be advised by the offshore administrator how to proceed. In most cases the claimant would contact the insurance company, probably through his attorney and would be instructed with regard to the procedure followed by this company in this regard.

In most cases the attorneys for the company would be unlikely to settle claims but would require that the claimants come to the islands and file in the Cayman courts. This alone would have a detrimental effect on the hopes of any claimant getting satisfaction from pursuit of a claim without just cause. He would have to be very sure of winning before he would be willing to go to a foreign jurisdiction to pursue his claim.

Possibility of Excess Coverage and Excess Limits

There would be times when a particular doctor or professional might want excess coverage or additional coverage in the form of specific riders to the policy. The rates set for these riders would be set by the underwriting committee in consultation with the insured so that the intent and purpose of the rider are clear. Funds paid to the company for excess coverage would be segregated and would be invested separately and would go into the premium recapture program after one year.

All other paid in premiums would remain in the company and invested by the company for four years before the unused premium would be available for premium recapture. This would create a separate pool of capital that would be invested on a short term basis and would be available only as collateral for other investments the committee may chose to make.

The Premium Recapture Concept

The most important single element of this insurance concept is the fact that the premium payer has the right to choose what shall happen to the unused and excess premium that is allocated on the company books for refund or recapture. After four years of continuous coverage the company will have sufficient funds to meet its ongoing obligations and will be ready to refund or rebate that portion of the paid in premium that has not been used or is not needed. This amount has been set at 40% of the annual premium depending on the exposure of the company, its history of claims and its investment policy.

Additionally, as a rule 90% of the excess premium paid for the rider outlined above would be eligible for the recapture program at the end of each year. This would mean after the first year if there is no change in the premium paid for the coverage it would amount to an immediate pass through to the designated recipient of this rebate.

Clearly, a prudent doctor would not like to receive a rebate of his insurance premium that has already been deducted as a proper business expense. Since, to accept the rebate would require him to declare the money as income and make that again subject to excessive tax. His option is to choose not to take any rebate but to allow this to be paid to the stockholder who has become indirectly associated with his ability to purchase this insurance in the first place through his membership in the affinity group.

The Source and Application of Funds

The board of directors of the offshore company formed in the Isle of Man give our client the specific responsibility with regard to the source and application of funds. Funds paid to the company, from the insurance company, for any reason fall under his responsibility. He is, in fact, securing funds for investment from an independent insurance company.

> This would mean that any unused premium or excess premium would be paid at the proper time to the Isle of Man company for which he works as managing consultant and would thus become investment income available to the company under his management. He would then continue under his agreement with the company to invest the funds and to compound its offshore assets into a sizable company with good investment track record.

The Foreign Grantor Trust

Since the insurance company is a foreign entity and is not under the control of any United States citizen, the insurance company could create a foreign grantor trust with segregated accounts. The foreign grantor trust could be used to hold all disbursements by the company from the unused premium account.

This would create a situation where the trust could then name a U.S. citizen as beneficiary of the trust and under Revenue Ruling 69-70 all funds paid to the U.S. citizen would be not subject to tax.

The Rights to the Benefits

If you have read this book this far you know that we, at Intercon Associates put more emphasis on the benefits that money can buy over the accumulation of money. Of course, one can gain more pleasure sitting on the sand in the city of Nice or skiing the Alps of France than he could laying in a pile of cash or standing on the biggest pile of money he could accumulate.

The pleasures of life are paid for with the funds accumulated or those directly or indirectly under your influence or control. If your responsibility on the staff of a foreign company is the source and application of funds, clearly much pleasure can be available to you in your application of those funds in fulfilling your responsibility.

The funds in the Isle of Man company are not subject to tax. Therefore there is no deductible or non-deductible criteria to which you submit the expenditure. You spend the money as you see fit, subject of course, to the approval of the board of directors or the trustee. The bank account is under the control of the bank, the administrator and the managing consultant. Money cannot be spent without your consent.

Income to the insurance company is under the direction of the company board of directors. You or your clients could serve on that board of directors because in no case can five or more have complete power over the company, so we will comply with U.S. tax law. The bank accounts of the insurance company are under the control of the board of directors and the administrators. The board of directors will have constant and continual oversight.

The Issue of Asset Protection

In the last analysis we have a combination of entities each designed to accomplish an important part of our international asset protection and investment program. Each is independent and each is a profit center in its own right. The insurance company offers standard insurance protection with the added advantage of acting in some ways as a mutual company, in that prudent management will create benefits to the stockholders.

The stockholders are the companies that are created for the use of the U.S. client under very careful rules that allow the client to be a consultant to the company without gaining control that would make it a controlled foreign corporation under the United States tax rules. This then creates a proper scheme where the tax deducible payment of insurance premium can ultimately bring benefits in the form of investment capital that can indirectly provide benefits to the insured beyond his wildest dreams.

The smart company owner setup an international business on the Isle of Man...

14
Your Right To Privacy, the Phantom Freedom

The Invasion of Your Privacy through Computer Data Banks and Credit Reporting

Our fight has just begun! The 21st century will bring some incredible changes in the way we live because of easy access to information about each of us. The computer revolution, with its massive ability to store information easily and the difficulty in erasing damaging information from your file, may affect not only how you live, but where you live and what you are able to buy.

In 1989 and on through the early 1990's, the news media began to show some interest in the far reaching invasion of privacy that is affecting the freedoms of the citizens of the United States. Several papers throughout the nation ran stories about how easy it is with computer banks to find out almost anything about any one of us. Much of the information that follows was taken from the San Francisco Chronicle, Friday, June 2, 1989.

If you thought your finances were private, think again. Financial data about you is being collected, analyzed and sold without your knowledge in unsettling new ways by banks, credit card companies, credit bureaus, private searchers, and direct marketing firms.

I first became aware of computers' data base awesome power during the Reagan campaign, in 1976. I was a

161

statewide volunteer for that effort and saw firsthand the ability of *direct mail marketing* to target specific households for mailing. They were able to select households in a certain income bracket, who lived in a certain zip code area, who drove certain types of cars and who sent their children to certain private schools.

It was an awesome demonstration of the ability of this new multi-billion dollar information exchange. Using computers and high speed data networks, they can literally learn how much money you make, the balance on your mortgage, where you shop, which bills you've paid, your alimony payments and much more. Increasingly, computer models using this data are helping to make snap judgments about whether you will get a job, credit, insurance or a place to live.

What follows is a general summary of what the news media reported (Summer, 1989) regarding the power of the credit reporting industry to invade your privacy. As is was reported, often there was no concern of your privacy. My readers, however, will see the libertarian view of the loss of personal freedom, and the invasion of privacy. Banks and credit bureaus argue that computerized credit reports and other data bases prevent fraud and are well-guarded against abuse. Except, the technical ability to gather and swap such data is outstripping data privacy laws enacted in the early 1970s, according to a growing chorus of privacy experts, civil liberty's groups and lawmakers. "The notion of financial privacy becomes largely an illusion," declared David Linowes, a well-known privacy expert at the University of Illinois in Urbana and the former chairman of the U.S. Privacy Protection Commission.

Consider this: Many records including individual credit reports used to measure consumer worthiness for a new loan contain errors or omissions that can be instantly repeated on thousands of computers. TRW, the nation's largest credit bureau, acknowledges that one-quarter (25%) to one-third (33%) of the people who ask to see their credit files find at least one error.

Safeguards against unauthorized access to data are not foolproof. Armed with $40, a name, address, and Social Security number, a citizen with no more credentials than a reporter can obtain a complete credit report on another individual with few problems. He can gain access to TRW's massive computer base even though both TRW and the credit agency may later say the incident was due to a lapse in enforcing their own rules of confidentiality. Credit bureaus, and even the government, increasingly sell lists of names culled from their files and are finding other ways to market their data and computing power.

Risk Models

TRW, for example, uses public data to estimate consumers' income to compile mailing lists of credit-worthy people that might be attractive to direct marketing firms. It also has a new *risk model* that figures the probability of delinquencies or bankruptcies by screening out consumers who look as if they may become deadbeats, those with what TRW terms marginal payment habits.

Banks, traditionally among the most secretive about customer information, also share account information in some ways. The last major survey of major banks, conducted by the University of Illinois a decade ago, found that they all disclose information about depositors and borrowers to those granting credit, and one-fourth (25%) also give information to landlords. Typically, the bank would reveal the approximate balance in the individual's account.

Linowes, who commissioned the Illinois study, says little has changed in the intervening 10 years. In fact, banks and credit card issuers sometimes even brag about how closely they monitor customer accounts. We have all seen the Citicorp Credit Card ad where a bank employee on the alert for stolen cards calls a customer to point out an unusual number of charges. The customer, who had rung up the charges himself, is grateful for Citicorp's concern rather than being upset at the intrusion.

American Express last year received some negative publicity when it admitted checking a new customer's bank account without their knowledge even though a bill was not due, simply because the customer had charged an unusually high amount on their card that month. The company now calls the whole incident an employee mistake and insists that it does not routinely snoop in customer's bank accounts, although it is legally authorized to do so by the fine print in the credit card application.

Quick Verification

Despite potential abuses, most experts agree, computerized checks on financial data have generally improved the way credit is granted in America. It was once difficult to verify good credit records quickly, especially across state lines. "If you want the ability to buy an automobile without cash, you're going to go for a loan and be very pleased there is a credit bureau out there to say you are a good risk," said one credit bureau executive.

Dominated by three major companies TRW, CBI/Equifax, and Trans Union these credit information bureaus maintain massive data bases containing more than 600 million individual credit files. Their reports contain such information as credit cards, credit limit, and credit history; other outstanding debts, bankruptcies, tax liens; and other negative court judgments. In some cases, the reports include your place of employment and salary.

Those who grant credit, such as banks and credit card issuers, are a credit bureau's main subscribers. Also, information is made available to collection agencies, insurance companies, private detectives, landlords, law enforcement agencies and, increasingly, employers trying to weed out bad hires. Some 42% of Fortune 500 companies recently surveyed by author Linowes said they collect information on employees without informing them.

Federal Safeguards?

The Fair Credit Reporting Act, enacted in 1970, put many safeguards into the system. For example, individuals' credit reports should only be legally disclosed to grant credit or another legitimate business purpose. Credit bureaus also are obliged to try to correct errors on such reports, but problems are common.

A Palo Alto, California social worker went to TRW's Foster City offices to dispute errors on her report that she said included an incorrect water bill for $300. She expects a six (6) to eight (8) week delay in financing a furniture purchase as she tries to get the water company to correct the error. This adds hardship to the case and in some cases makes the credit bureau liable for damages. Such problems are bound to continue, due to the explosion in computers and new databases.

In a report issued recently, the American Civil Liberties Union argued for overhauling privacy laws. It said the current laws have been overwhelmed by advanced information technology that gives institutions the powers "to instantly examine, compare, verify, and most importantly, link information in separate data bases."

In recent years, a new industry has begun to surface, one of Credit Repair. Many individuals whose credit report shows certain negative factors have elected to hire specialists in credit report repair to do anything legally possible to remove all negative ratings from the report. This is especially useful if the individual now needs to purchase a home or make some other large investment where a clear credit report is essential to the success of the application approval.

DMV Records

The government is also helping spread more information into private hands. For example, R. L. Polk Co., a well-known data service company, pays $700,000 to the California Department of Motor Vehicles (DMV) each year to buy all vehicle registration information and rent it to mail-order merchants.

Another example is the proposal for Medicare to put, now confidential, prescription data into computers that are used in most American drugstores. "We are very concerned about putting such sensitive personal information on-line with 52,000 pharmacists," said Janlori Goldman, an ACLU staff attorney specializing in privacy.

Such fears are spreading to lawmakers who are concerned about civil liberties. Earlier in 1989, Congress stopped the Social Security Administration from proceeding with its plan to cross-check 140,000,000 Social Security numbers with the numbers in TRW's 300 million-file database. Assemblywoman Gwen Moore, District-Los

Angeles, has introduced a bill in the state legislature that would require anyone using a computer to collect or distribute personal information to first notify the person about whom the information is being collected. This is a good first step.

However, the bill exempts companies from notifying people who have voluntarily given information to a business or agency. Although the law would exempt public utilities, local governments, credit bureaus, banks and newspapers, it would affect private detectives, research firms and computer hackers. It clearly does not go far enough to protect your right to privacy.

The New Breed

One new business that would be affected is Super Bureau Inc., a Monterey, California–based company that represents a new breed using computers to access credit bureaus, court records, voter registration files, land records, DMV files and a variety of other public records. "I think this concern over privacy is overblown," said Ned Fleming, Super Bureau's President. "These people have read one too many spy novels." For the most part, Fleming said, his company simply uses computers to quickly gain information from records that are already open to the public. As for tapping into confidential credit records, Fleming said he ensures that his clients have a legitimate business purpose before they receive such information.

Credit bureaus and the Direct Marketing Association, which represents users of computerized mailing lists, stress that lists derived from individual credit files are shared only with legitimate users under tightly controlled conditions. TRW, for example, seeds some sensitive lists with fictional

167

names and TRW addresses to find out who has improperly shared names.

Financial Redlining

Nonetheless, we should be concerned about financial-redlining. That is not offering or flatly denying credit based on non financial or on potentially misleading information. Obviously, a bank may not want to offer a credit card to someone on the verge of declaring bankruptcy. But such judgments sometimes are based on misleading and incorrect information.

Take TRW's new Risk Model to predict which customers may declare bankruptcy. TRW's Vice President for target marketing, Dennis Benner, said the scoring techniques used were proprietary. Then, he admitted, the decision depends in part on "things that don't necessarily relate to credit. Such as some demographic data."

What Happened to Your Inalienable Right to Privacy?

As you can see, a devastating assault is being made on your personal and financial freedom. The threat has never been greater. The attack is evident everywhere: attorneys' offices are being raided without warning; Customs Agents are searching passengers leaving the country and warning them about carrying cash; your foreign mail is being opened; and bank tellers are being ordered to report suspicious transactions. If you display your wealth by the house you live in or the car you drive, you could be the subject of professional thieves. You must fight to keep your assets from being stolen or sued or taxed away.

In a recent ruling the U. S. Supreme Court in United States vs. Miller said, "Individuals have no expectation of privacy when they reveal their financial affairs to another party." Yet it is nearly impossible to live in a cashless credit connected society without revealing this information to someone. Try to get a loan from the bank without giving them a copy of your latest tax return.

This information is then put into the computers for general distribution to anyone who asks. Justice Lewis Powell said, "The depositor takes the risk, in revealing his affairs to another, that the information will be given to the government." The Supreme Court has determined that your garbage is not private and agencies of the government can use your garbage to incriminate you. This new decision includes information which your physician, psychiatrist, attorney, CPA, etc., may discard as garbage.

IRS Code Section 7602

Gives the IRS the authority to look into the private financial lives of the U.S. Citizen including bank accounts, investment holdings, real estate holdings, partnerships, business accounts, retirement accounts, and any activity that involves the use of cash or debt instruments. That is not all!

IRS Code Sections 6001, 6011, and 6012 and their regulations

State that the U.S. citizen must file a return or statement for any tax the U.S. citizen may be responsible for, and must surrender to the IRS any documents requested.

IRS Code Section 6109 and its regulations

State that U.S. citizens must show their social security numbers on all documents they file. IRS codes allow reporting information on U.S. citizens to the Department of Justice, or other federal agencies, as provided by law. They may also give this information to cities, states, the District of Columbia, and United States commonwealths or possessions to carry out tax laws. This information may be given to foreign governments because of tax treaties.

IRS Codes Section 601.701 and Section 552 of Title S of the U.S. Code (Freedom of Information Act)

States that the public generally, or any member thereof, shall be afforded access to information or records in the possession of the IRS.

The U.S. government has been the most active, among the industrialized nations of the world, in secret negotiations for a multilateral treaty (INTERFIPOL), of the Organization for Economic Cooperation and Development (OECD) and the Council of Europe. This treaty, among other things, will require that any country, that is a party to the treaty, use its domestic internal police powers to collect taxes and apprehend suspected tax avoiders of any other country, that is a party to the treaty, anywhere in the world.

Fortunately, at this point few countries have signed on to the final draft. In time, we can expect many to do so and then international asset diversification and offshore business structures will be essential to privacy and profitable business activity.

The Bank Secrecy Act

This act, officially titled the Financial Record Keeping, Currency and Foreign Transactions Reporting Act, is the most far-reaching act of its kind ever enacted. The act requires that all U.S. banks maintain copies of deposit slips and both sides of all checks over $100. In addition, banks must keep a permanent record of any loan over $5,000 and must notify the treasury department directly of any deposit or withdrawal of more than $10,000. (Today, 18 years later, a $3,000 limit on unreported withdrawals has been proposed.)

The act requires banks to record the social security number of anyone opening any type of new account. They are required to turn into the treasury department the name of anyone who fails to provide this information within 45 days after the account has been opened. The act makes far reaching changes in the treatment of foreign bank accounts. All such accounts must now be reported. Any deposits in foreign banks that total $10,000 including interest during any part of a calendar year must be reported. Violation of this regulation is considered tax evasion and is a federal felony.

The act requires the U.S. citizen to report any interest or dividends received from any sources, including foreign, that exceeds $400. In addition the citizen must report the existence of a foreign account, the creation of a foreign trust in which the U.S. citizen was a grantor, or the transfer of assets to a foreign trust.

Foreign accounts must be identified by filing Treasury Form 90-22. This form is sent directly to the Treasury Department in Washington, D.C. not your regional IRS office. Currency controls were also imposed under the Bank Secrecy Act. It requires individuals transporting currency

171

and certain monetary instruments valued at more than $5,000 across U.S. borders to notify the U.S. Treasury via a Treasury Form 4790. Violators risk confiscation of any funds discovered, plus a fine of up to $500,000 and as much as five years in prison.

The act required banks, savings and loans, money market accounts, and security firms to report interest earned by clients on IRS Form 1099. The IRS Form 1099 is the most insidious regulation that has affected the freedom of U.S. citizens in this century. Unlike other IRS regulations that require the individual to report his or her income, this act requires each of us to report our expenditures and to whom they were paid. We must include in that report the social security number of the recipient. This essentially makes each of us a reporting agency of the IRS.

The Government Uses the Bank Secrecy Act to Erode Your Privacy

One of the first casualties of the Bank Secrecy Act was, not surprisingly, bank secrecy. With the volume of records U.S. banks were required to maintain, it was almost certain that, given enough "fishing" by the IRS, incriminating evidence against any of their depositors could be found. Government investigators routinely look into the bank accounts of leftists, people who advocate "revolutionary" social or political changes, and just about everyone who opposes the current administration or taxing authority. The effect of the Privacy Act has been negligible. Test yourself: When was the last time a government agency contacted you and informed you that it was using data for any purpose other than for which it was intended?

The Treasury
Enforcement Communications System

In order to enforce the currency control aspects of the Bank Secrecy Act, the U.S. Customs Service set up a computer network known as the Treasury Enforcement Communications System (TECS). A TECS terminal is placed, virtually at every major port of entry to the United States. When your name is entered into the system, TECS will report the following:

- If you are a convicted tax evader.

- If you are listed on the National Crime Information Center data base.

- If you are a suspected drug dealer.

- If you are suspected or have been convicted of smuggling or other black market offenses.

- If you are wanted for any criminal offense.

- If you are suspected in removing cash from the United States in violation of the Bank Secrecy Act.

Of course, the uses to which TECS can be put are always expanding. One government insider states that the TECS computer is now programmed to construct computerized profiles of individuals suspected of money laundering, drug smuggling, etc. By answering a few simple questions at the terminal, the customs agent can make an almost instantaneous decision whether or not to detain someone who appears to fit the profile.

173

The Deficit Reduction Act of 1984

Even after the passage of the Bank Secrecy Act, U.S. national deficits continued to rise and the underground economy to thrive. Legislative efforts were made to tighten the noose still further.

Travel is recorded by the Treasury Department to monitor any movement of its citizens. Plans are underway to read license plates by computer to know where you are and where you have been.

Passports will not be issued to anyone who has failed to file their tax returns. Taxpayer clearance is now required before your passport can be renewed. This list contains anyone who has not paid their income tax when due. Every applicant for a new passport, or renewal of an existing passport, will be required to file a tax preference form that will eventually require an IRS approval to travel. Disputes with the IRS will result in the loss of travel privileges outside the United States while the dispute is being resolved through the tax court. This could take years.

This regulation has created increased interest in a second passport, which could be used in place of the one that is recorded in the computer. Many countries are willing to issue a passport to investors or short-term residents without the requirement that you renounce your present citizenship.

Enormous progress has been made by the U.S. government in a form of computer technology termed "cross–matching". This technique permits a computer user to gather unrelated bits of information and put them together in order to identify trends.

Cross-matching was first used by the IRS to identify individuals involved in Welfare fraud and similar offenses.

The administration aggressively expanded the use of this technique to identify those who were delinquent on student loans. The administration was not content to simply stamp out welfare fraud and call in delinquent student loans. It lobbied vigorously for legislation that would use Social Security numbers to link dozens of government data bases.

The Deficit Reduction Act of 1984 enabled various government agencies to improve their data processing capabilities immensely. Customs upgraded its TECS system. The Secret Service wrote a program that constructs a "computer profile" to identify would-be assassins. Unquestionably, the biggest beneficiary of the Deficit Reduction Act is the IRS.

The act allowed the IRS to create a *debtor master file*. So far, the debtor master file lists nearly one million people who owe money to various government agencies. The IRS even buys lists from direct mail companies to find out if the spending habits of targeted individuals match their reported incomes. The purpose of the debtor master file is to "withhold tax refunds" owed to borrowers who have defaulted on federal loans. The debtor master file includes reports by credit companies (i.e., TRW) which monitor your payment profiles. These companies will tell you that they do not disclose information in your file to anyone who is not a client of the reporting agency. What they leave unsaid is that the IRS, FBI, DEA, CIA, and nearly every other government agency has an active client status with each credit reporting company.

Application for credit (auto, home, credit cards, etc.) are routinely checked by computer search to determine if credit applications contain information that has not been reported to the government on federal tax or information returns. State income tax authorities also began their own efforts to root out "tax cheating" (the act encourages states to construct cross-matching data networks so that they may "compare notes" and identify individuals who fail to pay state taxes.) All 50 states now receive computer tapes with federal tax information directly from the IRS. Only Nevada refuses to sign a reciprocal agreement.

The primary result of the Deficit Reduction Act of 1984 was the formal acceptance by the U.S. government of the social security number as the numbering process for the *National Identity Card*. During the debate on this issue, a new permanent identity card was voted down during a Reagan cabinet meeting because one member of the outer circle of agency assistants noted that it was very similar to the Nazi identification number tattoo used by Adolf Hitler in World War II.

However, the new card, based on already existing social security numbers, would include a magnetic strip and computer bar graph for instant identity and "cross--matching". You would be required to present this I.D. card before banking, investing, travel, or using debit systems in the commercial sector. It is interesting that with this change came the rules requiring Social Security numbers for children, giving the government cradle-to-grave tracking of your personal affairs.

A government bureaucrat, or anyone else having access to government records, can compile a complete record of your real estate holdings, your tax returns, your medical records, and your credit history simply by entering your Social Security number into the appropriate data base. Then there was the statement from a retired IRS agent recently who said, "Give me your Social Security number and I can find out anything about you."

What Records are Kept on You?

The following records are routinely kept on virtually every U.S. citizen by Federal, State and Local Governments:

- Birth Certificates
- Census Records
- Court Records
- Death Certificates
- Deeds
- FBI Records
- Federal Income Tax returns
- Local Tax returns
- Marriage Certificates
- Medical histories (public hospitals)
- Military Benefits received
- Motor Vehicle License

- Motor Vehicle Registration
- Passports
- Police Records
- Professional Licenses
- School Record
- Social Security Benefits received
- Social Security Taxes paid
- State Income Tax returns
- Unemployment Compensation received
- Veterans Benefits received
- Welfare payments received

The following private firms maintain computerized files that, in many cases, are freely accessible by federal agencies, as well as any other person or agency who wants to discover your personal data:

- Banks
- Brokerage houses
- Car Dealers
- Churches
  (contributions for purposes)
- Clubs
- Credit bureaus
- Doctors
  (including Psychiatrists)
- Employment agencies

- Financial institutions
- Genealogical bureaus
- Insurance companies
- Investment funds
- Mail order firms
- Mortgage companies
- Organizations

TRW has admitted in court under oath that they maintain over 300 million files on U. S. citizens. This is very interesting when you realize there are only 250 million men, women, and children in the United States.

The Tax Reform Act of 1986

Most U.S. citizens believe the Tax Reform Act of 1986 simply adjusted tax rates and changed some rules concerning deductibility of certain types of expenses. In fact, buried deep in the act is a virtual privacy invasion blitz, the effects of which will continue to be felt long after the tax adjustments it authorized are forgotten.

1. For starters, the act requires that all children be assigned social security numbers.

As noted earlier, together with the provisions of the Deficit Reduction Act of 1984, which sets up a nationwide Social Security number tracking system among government agencies, this provision assures a cradle-to-grave identification card for every American from the moment he or she is born.

Failure of the parents to register their child will result in the loss of dependent deductions for tax purposes and the potential loss of privileges to the child through social, education, and welfare programs.

2. The act stipulates that as of January 1, 1987, all real estate transactions must be reported to the IRS to prevent "under reporting" of real estate gains.

These transactions are to be reported on magnetic tape to "make IRS processing speedier."

A national IRS data base listing every homeowner in the United States is now in place. If you move residency or change addresses, you must notify the government agencies, DMV, IRS, licenses, etc., usually within 10 to 45 days.

A new form, IRS 1099B, has been developed to be filed by the real estate broker. It will give all the information on the sale of domestic property, including the seller_and the buyer with their tax identification numbers.

Under tax reform, all interest from Municipal Bonds must be reported, even though such interest is tax-exempt.

Why would the government make such a provision unless there was a plan at some future point to tax such income?

3. Perhaps the most insidious aspect of TRA '86 is a provision that requires the IRS to investigate a return free tax system.

This could result in a tax system without your knowledge or consent. In other words, the IRS, now that tax reform has almost totally eliminated tax deductions, could prepare your tax return simply by adding up all income that has been reported to it and subtracting the few deductions that are still allowed. Then, using an electronic bank wire, the IRS would simply deduct the amount of tax due from your bank account.

Similarly, by looking up your credit card number, the IRS would simply wire itself a cash advance at your expense. Since all U.S. bank accounts and credit cards are already identified by your social security number, the technical obstacles to the return free tax system are not very formidable.

In a national emergency, the IRS could quickly deduct, say, 20% of the funds in every bank account in the United States. This would be an advance to the government on future tax obligations. It would be up to the individual citizen to prove the taxes were not owed. TRA'86 is a grim reminder of the determination of the U.S. government to utterly destroy privacy. In fact, as will be noted later, since 1985 the U.S. government has been acting under a general state of emergency as outlined in Executive Order Number 12532.

The Computer Matching and Privacy Protection Act and the Electronic Privacy Act

It should certainly be clear at this point that a Federal Law containing the word **privacy** usually acts to invade rather than protect it. Proposed legislation now before Congress is no exception.

The Computer Matching and Privacy Act will give the government absolute authority and discretion to wiretap phones and plant bugs in homes and businesses without the knowledge or consent of those being monitored. It would also permit the government to directly tap private data banks that contain personal, financial, health, or other information.

As the U.S. government grows increasingly powerful, initiatives are now being taken by individual federal agencies without the explicit approval of Congress. In many cases, these plans pose as serious a threat to individual liberty and financial privacy as legislation actually passed by Congress.

The National Security Agency, a super secret arm of the federal government, is capable of monitoring phone calls made between the United States and foreign nations. Recording of individual conversations may be automatically triggered by certain key words, indicating that what is being discussed is of security (or tax) interest to the U.S. government.

In June 1987, the National Crime Information Center (NCIC) proposed the creation of a national computerized file that would permit federal, state, and local law enforcement agencies to exchange information on people

181

who are suspected of a crime but have not been charged. Under the proposal, the NCIC would have electronic access to records of the Internal Revenue Service, the Securities and Exchange Commission, the Immigration and Naturalization Service, the Social Security Administration, the Department of State, and the passport office. Republican Don Edwards (District California) described these actions as "...a revolutionary change, permitting law enforcement agencies to pass around investigative information, much of it rumors and gossip, over a national computer system run by Big Brother."

The Change of Money

For many years, hard money advocates and those who are pushing for return to the gold standard for the United States have reported that the U.S. government is going to recall all of the "greenbacks" and issue new money. No one has officially confirmed that fact; however, there is a body of circumstantial evidence that seems to indicate not only is it possible but there may be some good reasons for doing so.

The Bureau of Engraving and Printing is constructing a 300,000-square-foot facility near Fort Worth, Texas to produce sophisticated *counterfeit-proof money*. This is necessary, says the Bureau, to cope with the newest generation of color copiers. These new copiers are said to render almost perfect copies of today's greenbacks.

The new money will also trip airport security devices. Don't expect to take any quantity of money overseas with any expectation of privacy after the new money comes out. What a better way for the government to collect a multi-billion-dollar windfall than to introduce this new currency all at once and set a specific date after which the "old money" will no longer be legal tender?

The most convenient place for the switch to be made would be banks. You can imagine the scenario: After you produce a photo ID and a social security card, a helpful IRS agent politely asks you to account for the origin of every dollar that you brought to exchange. If you couldn't produce immediate proof, a certain percentage would immediately be deducted for **taxes**. If you turned in more than your **share** of cash, you would immediately be targeted for further investigation.

It is likely that the U.S. government will combine a currency switch with an instant devaluation of its currency to about one-quarter (25%) of its current value. This action would dramatically reduce the nation's trade deficit and has a devastating effect on anyone who had not already set up accounts denominated in foreign currencies.

By identifying individuals selling gold, the IRS is taking the first step toward a new campaign of gold confiscation. There is clear precedent for such action. On at least three occasions, the U.S. government impounded private stocks of gold: during the Revolutionary War, during the Civil War, and in 1933, immediately after the inauguration of President Franklin D. Roosevelt. The penalty for non-compliance with the most recent executive order was a $10,000 fine or 10 years in prison.

This time, once confiscation begins the government won't need to appeal to public conscience. After a limited period, during which the public could **voluntarily** turn over gold and other precious metals to the government, it could simply send armed Treasury Agents to the homes of suspected **hoarders**. Whatever wasn't submitted voluntarily could be taken by force.

What's Coming

Your attorney, your accountant, even your bank clerk will be obligated to testify against you, under oath, becoming Federal informants. The new IRS computer system will monitor everything you do. Wages will be a credit to your account. Purchases will be debits. If you buy a toothbrush, "Big Brother" will know about it.

Basic accounts will be identified by personal I.D. codes, which will be tied into the social security codes. At the touch of a button the U.S. Treasury or any officer of the court will be able to tabulate the sum total of all your savings accounts and personal holdings plus transactions. You will be subject to incredible tax probes. Your investments, your income, even your private life will be laid bare before the IRS. The IRS Form 1040 is becoming an "information return" to eliminate privacy of the U.S. citizen.

In short, virtually every aspect of your life, financial and personal, will be traceable by some agency of the U.S. government. Doesn't it bother you to know that, for about 10 cents, anyone can purchase a mailing list that identifies you by the type of car you own, the credit cards you use, the value of your home, or your political beliefs?

The Paper Wall

A major effort is underway to destroy bank secrecy laws and offshore bank activity, which will result in a substantial loss of economic freedoms for all Americans. Some proposed legislation includes:

- Authorizing customs agents to increase body and luggage searches on anyone leaving the United States.

- Treating loans from foreign sources as taxable income.

- Treating loans from insurance policies as taxable income.

- Requiring a visa for Americans traveling to tax–neutral countries.

- Denying tax benefits for banks incorporated in tax–neutral countries that are owned by a U.S. citizen.

Government by Emergency Decree

To prepare for the possibility of nuclear war, Congress has set up emergency legislation that, in time of war, permits the President to declare a "state of emergency" and assume extraordinary powers. Unfortunately, these powers are not specifically reserved for wartime. They can be invoked for virtually any situation the President deems to an emergency. They contain provisions that would instantly transform the United States into a totalitarian state, including the total abolition of civil liberties and the confiscation of privately held wealth. This vast range of powers confers authority on the President to rule the nation by decree and virtually suspend "due process of law" under the Constitution.

In fact, since September 1985, the United States has been operating under a State of Emergency. We are not at war. Except, on September 9, 1985, President Ronald Reagan issued Executive Order 12532, which began as follows.

"I, Ronald Reagan, President of the United States of America, find that the policies and action of the Government of South Africa constitute an unusual

and extraordinary threat to the foreign policy and
economy of the United States and hereby declare a
National Emergency to deal with that threat."

Today, hardly anyone remembers Executive Order
12532. Executive Order 12532 opens a Pandora's box of
Emergency Powers that the President can assume at any
time. Using emergency powers, the President may do any of
these things:

- Seize property.

- Organize and control the production of industrial
  and agricultural goods.

- Seize commodities that are being hoarded.

- Assign military forces abroad without the consent of
  Congress.

- Institute Martial Law.

- Close all banks and regulate withdrawals from
  banks.

- Prohibit unauthorized transportation.

- Prohibit use of private telephones and other communication equipment.

Now that a State of Emergency has been declared,
more than 500 secret emergency orders may be invoked by
the President via an executive order. Two of the more interesting emergency orders the President might invoke are
Emergency Banking Regulation 1 and Emergency
Preparedness Functions.

- Emergency Banking Regulation 1

  This executive order provides for the total power of the
  U.S. banking system by Presidential decree. It restricts
  cash withdrawals "except for those purposes and
  amounts for which cash is customarily used." It prohibits

cash withdrawals altogether "where there is reason to believe that such withdrawal is for the purpose of hoarding." A bank loan is also forbidden "unless it is established that the purpose is in the best interest of the public."

- Emergency Preparedness Functions

This starts with total censorship, including all "devices capable of emitting electromagnetic radiation," (i.e.,telephones, CB radios and personal computers). It continues with the "utilization of excess and surplus real and personal property." In other words, just about anything you own can be confiscated and sold by the federal government. Even banks are not forgotten. The order guarantees "liquidity" for banks in any circumstance. It also provides for the inflation such liquidity would almost certainly cause by freezing all prices and wages.

Freedom Isn't Free

Our freedom to simply be left alone to save and spend our own money as we choose has been seriously eroded. We must not be ashamed to vigorously exert our right to privacy. Consider the wording of the Fourth Amendment to the U.S. Constitution: "The right of the people to be secure in their persons, houses, papers and effects, against unreasonable searches and seizures, shall not be violated, and no warrants shall issue, but upon probable cause, supported by oath or affirmation, and particularly describing the place to be searched and the persons or things to be seized."

What is the Answer?

There is no need to allow this continued intrusion into your private financial affairs. You can achieve privacy by using a method that has been used by others since the early 1400s to guarantee their privacy. Through the use of international structures, including corporations, trusts, or banking arrangements, you can move yourself out of the jurisdiction of the U.S. government. Under current law, collecting against assets assumed to be yours properly held in a tax-free jurisdiction are beyond the reach of the IRS.

It is important that any structure be disconnected from the U. S. citizen. All structures must be put in place in such a way that you are not beneficially connected, or the long arm of the IRS will declare them to be yours and will tax you as if they were stateside entities.

15

Your Passport to International Profits and Offshore Asset Protection

Intercon Associates, Ltd.

Intercon Associates, Ltd., is primarily a consulting service that offers an analysis of a client's need for international small-business services, investment and asset protection services.

Working through carefully selected qualified domestic advisors, we meet with our prospective clients. At this time we discuss the opportunities that may exist for international asset protection and expansion of their business. We discuss the many options for capital accumulation and preservation through the use of foreign or domestic entities.

LAD Financial Service of Reno, Nevada is one of our affiliated domestic advisors. We work within this network of qualified asset protection and estate planners who accumulate the necessary data to advise the client locally and to send a meaningful referral to the international offices of Intercon Associates or one of our associated companies in Europe or the Caribbean for the actual formation and management of the foreign company or trust.

We recognize the fact that the United States citizen is limited in his access to offshore opportunities because of the IRS tax regulations that require taxes to be paid on world wide income that is linked to a United States citizen or business entity. It is therefore essential to any successful foreign program that the connecting factors be broken and that the United States citizen be free to act in the best interests of the company or trust.

When the structure is properly established it can be any kind of business or financial service. We strive to set up the company and to operate it in such a way that there are no residual problems for our clients.

We begin our relationship with each client by preparing a complete and detailed "Confidential International Business Plan" described later in this chapter. On the basis of the information given to us in your answers to our initial questionnaire we will design a specific program to fit the clients needs.

The Confidential International Business Plan

This is a very detailed 60 page business plan that outlines the design, creation, and client interaction with a foreign company or trust.

The following confidential international business plan table of contents virtually covers every aspect of company operations.

Table of Contents

- Annual officers and directors contract

- Corporate tax and accounting package

- Get the best return from company involvement

- Your company documents

- Problem of privacy

- Your interaction with the registered agent

- Your accounting records

- Breaking the connecting factor

- Letter of wishes

- Specific details on your company structure

- Sample articles of association and organizational minutes

The Need for Professional Estate Planning

The principals of Intercon Associates are active members of the International Tax Planners Association, the Offshore Institute, and the Association of Independent Business Managers, as well as members of the International Association of Financial Planners. We will use all of the resources at our disposal to create an effective and useful international business plan.

Our primary role is one of international business consult and company administration. We choose to work with several estate planners and attorneys who understand off shore integration and will work with our clients to review their estate planning needs and to set up these domestic structures.

Most suggested structures will begin with a foreign company. These purposes are accomplished much better if the structure is created from a foreign base. We then enter the picture with offshore administration coordination. The "Four Square" table that follows is designed to give you a clear understanding of the various options that are available to you.

Working closely with your domestic estate planner or asset protection consultant we are able to create a fully integrated plan that will make it possible to move your assets offshore and to use these assets at will to enhance your lifestyle and build a sizable foreign estate.

Four Square Analysis

Our clients' first objective is to successfully and profitably operate their international investment of marketing business and to legally earn the greatest possible **tax free** return.

In our research we noticed that virtually all of the asset protection and international investment programs offered in the United States have many features in common. We have tried to summarize these in the table that follows.

Each of the squares is separate and distinct from the other. Transactions between them are always at arms length, and always supported by contracts offering substance to the chosen form. Each has its own characteristics and its own relationship to the government. Each has its own type of business structures and can interact with the others.

You can see where the Intercon Associates system, beginning with the Hybrid Isle of Man company in the upper half of this table, can add additional entities in a modular fashion to build an effective international asset protection and estate planning fortress.

Intercon Associates begins its involvement with the entities found in the upper half of the four squares. We can add other elements as needed or in response to the needs generated by your domestic advisors. In all cases the formation of the entity is begun from a foreign jurisdiction and is unlinked to the United States citizen.

Many of our clients come to us with foreign source income and have no desire to bring this money directly into the United States and into our tax system. With these individuals the system is designed to create the foreign entity to avoid that unnecessary exposure.

Intercon Associates is a foreign offshore company with administrative offices in The Isle of Man, London, and Dublin. Intercon Associates does foreign company formation and administrative work on behalf of our clients in all parts of the world. We specialize in high net worth individuals from high tax jurisdictions.

As you carefully review the table that follows you will see the flow of money logically begins at the foreign offshore "piggy bank company." It is only subject to tax if it is brought into the United States as income or dividends subject to tax.

THE FOUR SQUARE TABLE

Foreign Entity or Trust	Foreign Holding Company
	(Piggy Bank Company)
Is established by a foreign entity	
May have U.S. Tax ID number	Is established by foreign entity
May do substantial U.S. business	Has no U.S. linkage
If so, file 1040NR	Has no U.S. tax
Generally has no taxable profit	Is established in tax haven
Has no U.S. connecting factor	Pays little or no tax on profit
Complete asset protection	Complete asset protection
Example	**Example**
Asset protection trust	Foreign investment company
Second level business trust	Offshore captive insurance company
Offshore charitable	Import/Export business
Irrevocable discretionary trust	Re-invoicing business
Foreign hybrid (IOM) company	International consulting business
	International leasing company
	Foreign hybrid (IOM) company
Domestic Entity	**Individual**
Is its own entity -- once removed	Has personal tax liability
Files its own tax forms	Assets are not protected from
(1120, 1041)	creditors
Offers first line asset protection	
Example	**Example**
"C" Corporation (Nevada)	Sole proprietor
First Level Business trust	"S" Corporation (Nevada)
Revocable Trust	Living Trust* (some protection)
Family Limited Partnership	Professional corporation
Irrevocable Asset Protection Trust	Professional pension plans
Charitable Temainder Trust	Personal investment accounts
	IRA

Our Eight Point Service Committment

InterconAssociates is a service oriented company. Our staff is dedicated to the concept of service, in so doing we provide the client with trouble free company management. This is our eight point service commitment.

1. As a direct result of our consultation with you and our analysis of your needs, we undertake to create or cause to be created certain domestic and foreign company and/or trust structures for your use. We instruct the directors of the company to appoint you to a position of responsibility and to give you complete responsibility with regard to the source and application of funds.

2. In order to train our clients in the use of the proper forms and the administration and management of their company structure, both domestic and foreign, if he is not already enrolled, we encourage each client to enroll in the Association of Independent Business Managers or a similar management organization. This will give exposure to the proper form and useful interactive techniques.

3. We retain the position of "Assistant Administrator" or trust "Protector" and in that capacity retain the responsibility for selection of suitable company or trust administrator or registered agent in the chosen country of domicile, and offer oversight with regard to the time charges that are charged to the company.

4. We create a definite break in the connecting factors between you and the foreign company by retaining unto Intercon Associates, Ltd., the responsibility for paying the fees to the country of domicile along with the annual standing charges and tax exempt fees.

5. Once a company is created for our clients, we are obligated to provide that business with ongoing support services. Therefore, we retain an interest in an investment advisory service in London, and make ongoing investment advisory services available to our consultants or clients.

6. We set up and maintain office facilities for your foreign company in London, where important records with regard to the company, such as the company charter, bylaws, and annual minutes are maintained for your convenience in a private location. Similar service is available in London for up to £1,800 per year. We include it in our service package at no additional cost.

7. We provide mail forwarding service for your company, as a part of that office package, so that you can confidently use the London office for receipt of certain mail that for one reason or another could not be delivered to the United States.

8. The phone is answered at the London office in a general manner and you can confidently ask your business associates to call you at that location. A message will be taken and will be faxed or mailed to the address you specify for contact in this country.

We Select the Best Registered Agent for You

Our clients second objective is to move a substantial portion of their assets into an offshore jurisdiction where these assets will be **safe, secure and protected** from the efforts of judgment creditors plaintiff's attorneys, and government collection agents

197

Intercon Associates is a foreign based company whose function is to negotiate with and set up certain international business structures to accomplish the objectives of the client in any suitable jurisdiction in the international marketplace. We do not simply buy the least expensive company or trust off the shelf.

Intercon Associates acts as an advocate or facilitator between its network of reliable company registered agents in whatever jurisdiction is selected for the company purpose and the client who is designated company employee with management responsibilities.

When a trust is used, we will also act as trust "protectors." A trust must have an independent adversarial trustee. We select that individual or company and as protectors are in a position to look after your interests. This is an essential element of the trust document that provides some indirect control by the settler. We provide that essential service to our clients.

We often set up a branch office for a client in another jurisdiction other than Europe or the Isle of Man. This can be set up in the Caribbean, the Far East, or any jurisdiction that is indicated as a result of our consultation as the best place for you to do business.

Since the company or trust is formed by Intercon all financial obligations to the country of domicile are assumed by Intercon thereby cutting cleanly all connecting factors to the client or employee of the company. This will explain why our fees may seem higher than others offering similar services.

This would mean that all assessments and fees due to the country, all fees due to the officers or directors, and all general operating charges are the responsibility of Intercon Associates. Included in the company payment of the quarterly fees to Intercon Associates are sufficient funds to keep the company current and viable at all times.

Minimum Capital for an Investment Company

Your answers to the general questions in the "Client Questionnaire" will give us a good overview of your situation. Additionally, since most of our clients think in terms of an investment company, this will tell us the amount of money you feel you could use to capitalize the foreign company.

As a rule of thumb, if you were considering less than $50,000, the income earned by the foreign company may be only sufficient to cover little more than the costs of operations. So other alternatives such as the maximum use of a domestic corporation or trust would need to be researched and recommended.

If your initial estimate is in excess of $100,000, we can be assured that prudent investment of this amount will create a good investment pool and you should do very well indeed. Obviously funds in excess of that amount since they accumulate and compound tax free can build a rather comfortable retirement nest egg.

Though the above statements assume earning less than ten percent, we should point out to you that the panel of investment advisors upon whose advice our clients rely, has established track records of investment programs that consistently earn well in excess of that amount, tax free to our clients' companies.

Criteria for Manufacturing
or Sales Company

Our clients third objective is to address their constitutional right to privacy. They intend to meet the first and second objectives without their business or personal activity being a matter of public record.

If the company is to be an international manufacturing or sales company, a totally different set of criteria applies. Clearly, any dollars diverted to the foreign company are dollars not paid to your business or to yourself here in the United States. This income is subject only to tax in the country of domicile and may even be free of any taxation. This can immediately effect the earning power and competitive position of the foreign company. Savings start with the first tax free dollar.

This sort of reasoning applies to commissions or contracts payable from a foreign source as well. These are dollars that should never be brought into the United States since your objective is to keep their existence confidential, make your company more competitive, and to indirectly enjoy the benefits of the company existence.

Finally, we frequently find a prospective United States client who has secretly and illegally maintained a foreign bank account in excess of the $10,000 allowed by the U.S. tax code. These individuals are worried and have good reason to be.

In today's sophisticated technical society such risks are unwise. Computer screening and information exchange treaties are uncovering hundreds of illegal accounts. These funds need to become a part of the foreign company assets as soon as possible. They are then legal and the client can sleep better at night. An international asset protection system must be designed and operated in such a way that the client can have complete confidence and constant peace of mind.

Essential Criteria of International Planning

Breaking the connecting factor remains the most important service that Intercon Associates offers its clients

The first criterion is to set up a structure that breaks the connecting factors, giving you complete asset protection while separating you from any connection that would generate tax liability for the United States citizen. We do not recommend that the United States citizen hold stock or serve as a director of the company that is formed for his use. His interests can be protected in the operation of the company.

One of the critical links to an individual is his signature on any official document. This can include minutes of the company, its bank mandate or checking or investment accounts. As a consultant to the company, our client makes recommendations that are submitted to the board of directors or to the company administrators for action. His position of responsibility will be honored and his recommendations will be activated. But, in no case can there be a signed document to require this action.

A properly structured entity that breaks these connecting factors will withstand any challenge by the courts or by the government in the event of an attempt to confiscate your assets. This is an essential element of asset protection. It can be done in a way that the client can feel confident in the security of his assets.

The Importance of the Rahman Decision

In 1990 an important case was decided in the Isle of Jersey that has an effect on all companies and trusts created worldwide. This was known as the Rahman Case.

In this case the court ruled that in order for a trust to be effective and not a **sham,** the settler must give complete discretionary control to the trustee. The trustee cannot be simply an accountant for the settler, with all decisions made by someone other than the person legally responsible for these decisions.

This serves to confirm our commitment to finding the best and most reliable trustee or company administrators in the off shore world to handle our company's affairs. We then must entrust them with certain responsibilities and then trust them to follow up on our suggestions or recommendations. We must learn to **trust the trustee.**

The Isle of Man "Hybrid Company"

The Isle of Man "Hybrid Company" is one of the best international structures available for asset protection.

Clearly, the most important single element in any foreign structure is the initial step. For this purpose we favor the use of an irrevocable discretionary trust, or the Isle of Man guarantee "Hybrid" company, which is in fact a form of trust relationship. We consider this to be the "Cadillac" of offshore planning.

A more detailed explanation of that company use is essential to your understanding of how the Intercon system works. This is something that can not be fully explained in a book. The details are fully explained in the "Confidential

International Business Plan." This is the primary purpose of that document for each of our clients.

It is essential in any offshore structure that is designed to withstand an inquisition by any government agency that the United States citizen be totally and completely unlinked from the company. Yet the client needs the assurance of the security of the company assets.

The proper use of the Hybrid company as described in Appendix I, "Isle of Man: A Business and Tax Haven" is critical to this concept. In essence, we must re-create the individual as a foreigner through the use of this unique company structure. Each individual who works with us is so re-created. The key element of your involvement with the Hybrid is that you are elected as an *associate member* with rights of distribution, but without the right to vote. This takes you out of the control loop but gives you the right to all the assets should the company ever be dissolved. This fact gives you the assurance of the security of any assets you may have assigned or loaned to the company.

You, acting as the CEO, dealing directly with the selected registered agent, are responsible for the source and application of funds. You alone are responsible for the assets of the company. No one else is given that responsibility and no disbursements can take place without your approval as the responsible employee.

The Use of Trusts or "BTO's"

From time to time advisors in the United States as well as other countries have recommended and promoted the use of trusts in estate and tax planning. There is no question that such entities are very useful and have been used for centuries by the very wealthy to accumulate and preserve their wealth.

Through the use of our system, integration of the trust is made more effective. As stated earlier, "A proper structure begins offshore and is not connected." Our offshore structure and unlinked management will only enhance the entire asset protection system. The creations and use of an asset protection or discretionary trust is easily done at any time in our relationship.

The Asset Protection Trust

> 1. Is designed to be neutral.
>
> 2. Effectiveness is in difficult access.
>
> 3. Trustee must have control.
>
> 4. Can create trustee liability.
>
> 5. Beware of sham.

Within the United States, high net worth individuals are often given the opportunity to place their assets into what is known as an Asset Protection Trust (APT). An asset protection trust is an entity that is established by a grantor, in this case the U.S. citizen, and is domiciled in a foreign jurisdiction. The fact that it may be established by a U.S. citizen as the grantor means that he will be taxed on the income earned by the trust and even though it is domiciled in a foreign country is essentially a U. S. trust for tax purposes. This makes it tax neutral in the eyes of the IRS.

Asset protection comes from the difficulty of any judgment creditor to gain access to the assets because of the foreign domicile. Most creditors including the federal

204

government will not pursue assets that are properly and legally placed in a foreign asset protection trust.

Care must be taken to give the trustee complete discretionary control of the assets as well as signature power on the accounts to avoid possibility of being called a sham. You should also bear in mind that the beneficiaries can bring claims against the trustee, even for unfortunate activity of the underlying company or domestic limited partnership.

We strongly believe that the Foreign Hybrid Company or irrevocable trust established by Intercon Associates a foreign entity, and made available to the client for his use is a much more effective asset protection tool and also offers enhanced safety, and tremendous tax advantages.

Asset protection means, "What you do not own or hold title to, your creditors cannot take from you."

The Selection of the Right Jurisdiction

The second criterion is, if necessary, to extend your business concept may be to include workable and beneficial arrangements in countries that have a double tax treaty with the United States thereby avoiding any withholding tax on interest, dividends, and royalties that is due from payments made to a tax haven.

There are many countries that have tax treaties with the United States that contain very favorable administrative loop holes. Our job will be to research these countries and to recommend the best possible jurisdiction to you.

Research is an essential part of the basic unit of the Intercon System. This is why we establish our foundation unit, the Hybrid "Piggy Bank" in the Isle of Man. From that base we can add additional modules that will enhance the overall system and legally avoid excessive taxation.

The Caribbean Option

An optional service offered by Intercon Associates, Ltd., is one most commonly used by United States offshore advisors. This is the offshore irrevocable trust with underlying company. One must be careful with this structure to be sure that there are no connecting factors that will create tax linkage to the United States.

It is especially true in the case of the declaration of trust that real powers be given to the trustee. Here again the effect of the Rahman decision can be seen. Entities that are created with no real substance in an offshore jurisdiction will be seen as a **sham** in any high tax jurisdiction that is attempting to break the shield of protection.

In addition to our basic business operations in Europe, Intercon Associates offers a less expensive service in the set up and operation of trusts with companies in tax free Caribbean jurisdictions. We offer the same types of business service in the form of operating companies. However, in most instances the Isle of Man Hybrid company or irrevocable trust is still valuable as the initial building block upon which your foreign empire can grow.

Another available option in the Cayman Islands is the use of the basic foreign offshore company whose stock is owned by an irrevocable declaration of trust with an independent trustee. This is the least expensive entity but as stated earlier offers the most possibility of challenge by the IRS or any other government agency.

We recommend that if a Turks and Caicos or Cayman company is to be used it be the operating subsidiary or branch of an Isle of Man Hybrid company to offer the greatest security and flexibility. If the client is once removed by way of the Isle of Man Hybrid or a foreign irrevocable trust there is less problem with government intervention in your private affairs.

Our services in the Cayman Islands are similar to those of the Isle of Man. We set up and operate the company on behalf of the client and appoint him to a powerful position of responsibility. We charge an ongoing quarterly fee for maintaining that break in connecting factors.

The cost of any offshore structure is directly proportional to the security and safety of the structure.

The Basis of Our Fee Structure

Fees paid to a foreign company or trust administrator should be based on services rendered and not on a percentage of assets in trust.

The basis of our fee structure is detailed below and will be further explained in consultation with you. Our fees will be specific to the company structure you will be operating. We will also include any possible interaction with a corporation or trust set up in the State of Nevada to easily access the United States market.

Intercon Associates, Ltd., will charge a basic flat fee to set-up the first company structure to initiate your entry into the offshore world. Well over half of this fee is paid out to our professional colleagues and business associates as necessary expenses in the set up of companies in the chosen jurisdiction.

There will also be an ongoing quarterly management fee that will be charged to your company. This quarterly fee includes all of the costs that are passed through to the resident agent, the country government offices, and the directors of the company, thereby breaking any connecting factors to the client.

This quarterly fee will cover the general operating costs outlined above as well as the features and costs associated with the London address for the newly formed company. Additionally, we are sure every client will need access to continuing consultation. We assume that he will use the services of our consultants at least 2 hours each quarter and include the fee for this consultation in the quarterly fee structure.

Finally, Intercon Associates, Ltd., continues to maintain a relationship with investment managers that are licensed with the NASD in the United States and FIMBRA in Great Britain. This allows us to offer outstanding investment opportunities to our clients. We continually receive investment suggestions from our network of world wide investment advisors and group of competent money managers.

This gives Intercon Associates, Ltd., the ability to offer offshore investment advisory service and to assist you in contact with other investment advisors or money managers for the investment of excess corporate funds and possible extensions of the structure to include new companies or trusts. Our objective is to keep the costs under control and to invest the excess funds in the company accounts in such a way that the company will be self-sustaining.

We are often asked to present a lecture on the subject of "Use of Offshore Entities for Privacy, Protection and Profit" at seminars and symposia around the United States and other countries of the world. We have learned that access to the international investment market is a primary concern of the most high net individuals.

Assuming Management Control of an Existing Company

Often we meet an individual who has purchased a company or trust and has had no meaningful follow-up. They seek our help. We are asked what the cost would be to assume management of an already existing offshore company or trust.

We are happy to take on this responsibility, however it may be necessary to modify the company organization in some way. Our cost of this service is based on our hourly rate and actual costs incurred. After the company is transferred to one of our selected administrators it then becomes one of the Intercon Associates, Ltd., group of companies and is thereafter responsible for ongoing quarterly fees.

Subsequent Modules as Your Company Grows

As a service to our existing clients Intercon Associates will establish whatever company or business trust organization the client requires in most of the tax haven jurisdictions of the world. This will allow for the government fees, administrative accounting, and original set up costs of any additional module. It is our intention to keep costs of service as low as possible. The company will then be subject to the ongoing quarterly maintenance fees.

The happy company owner enjoying all the benefits of a maximum tax-free profit.

16

And in Conclusion... a Golden Opportunity

All good things must come to an end. So, in conclusion, this final chapter is full of very useful ideas and explanations. Much of it is subtle and requires reading between the lines. Much additional information can only be fully explained in a personal consultation with a competent business and tax consultant. For this reason Intercon Associates and LAD Financial Services have met and decided to make a dramatic change in the way we do business. This is outlined later in this chapter.

First let us review "How and Why Americans Go Offshore". The first of the three reasons that spring to mind is the privacy that foreign administrators offer the business person. The second reason are the profits that can be earned in the foreign investment market with the excess earnings of a company operation. The third and most important reason is the protection that foreign operation offers the United States citizen.

As outlined in the chapter on captive insurance, our citizens in all walks of life are under siege by a system of courts and jurisprudence that is not only corrupt but designed to take from the rich and give to the poor or those who can claim poverty. The need for asset protection is the hottest topic on the lecture circuit this year. It has been for the last three years and with the prospect of the politics of

211

the 90's facing us, we know that this will be a major effort in the coming decade.

Let us look at some irrefutable facts:

• Fact #1: One person in four will face a major lawsuit during his business life. Today's judgments usually start at about $250,000 and rise rapidly into the millions. Many of these judgments outstrip the most generous insurance coverage and lead to financial devastation to the defendant. A legal defense even when innocent of charges can run from $50,000 to $75,000 and more! Your risk to liability goes up every year while your protection goes down. The costs rise while the coverage is reduced. This significantly increases the risk to everything you own.

• Fact #2: With the election of Bill Clinton (and his wife) to the White House we will see a dramatic increase in taxes imposed on individuals and businesses in the United States over the next few years. Taxes imposed on business leads directly to job loss. At a time in history when business is "down-sizing" this will lead to an exacerbation of the social problems and the expenses associated with that aspect of our society.

• Fact #3: The problems of the deficit are real. We cheer when congress lowers in a small way the projected rise in the coming years. This is fiscal folly. We must cut the deficit, not just reduce the rise of the deficit. Unless these annual increases in the national debt are brought under control the United States will not be able to pay the interest on the debt and meet the mandated entitlements that are in the law. This is clearly outlined in the book, "Bankruptcy 1995."

- Fact #4: Thousands of businesses and families are devastated by confiscatory taxes. The tax rate the middle class will pay over the next decade will be more than 50%. This includes all Federal, State and Local taxes. No country can long survive if the tax rate remains over 50% for any length of time. In addition the probate and estate taxes are once again under attack. If this is successful your best laid plans for passing your estate on to your heirs are gone. You can kiss it good-by and give everything to Uncle Sam.

- Fact #5: Virtually all of our assets are under attack. There was a time and there was a place where your personal residence and your pension plans were secure. This is no longer the case. Clever lawyers can now pierce most of the protective shields we have had available to us in the United States.

- Fact #6: Your personal and business privacy is virtually non-existent. The reporting requirements placed on our banks, on our businesses, and on ourselves require that every asset we have or in any way claim title to is open to public view. All government agencies know everything about you and can exchange this information with any other department including the IRS. Big Brother indeed knows all!

- Fact #7: Our banking system is in serious trouble. At last count, 1,100 out of 12,500 U.S. banks were in serious trouble. Over $1.5 Billion dollars on deposit in U.S. Banks is underinsured or uninsured by the Federal Deposit Insurance Corporation, The FDIC. United States citizens pride themselves in the security of the banking system because of this FDIC. What a shock it will be to find that the money they thought was secure is gone!

213

- Fact #8: Businesses are suing businesses like never before. From 1968 to 1988 contract cases were up 250%, bankruptcies were up 400%, and intellectual property, patents, copyright, and software piracy violations were up 280%. Businesses must create ways to move assets into a safe harbor or be prepared to share the wealth with their competitors.

- Fact #9: If you own a business you personally or your business could be paying tens of thousands of dollars each year in needless taxes. This book has taken great pains to help you understand that we are all in business in one way or another. With proper creation and use of foreign business structures the tax impact of your life can be legally reduced dramatically. It makes no sense to pay money to the government when, with a little legal structuring, you could spend it yourself any way you please.

- Fact #10: The ravages of divorce and family breakdown has a dramatic financial impact. Fifty percent of all marriages end in divorce. In a bill before the state legislature in California the wage earner with two children will be required to pay HALF of his or her income in child support. Clearly if this person is the wage earner for more than one family then this person will be between a rock and the hard place if this passes. The main question that needs to be asked and honestly answered is "What could this cost, my dependents, my estate and myself?" It might give us reason to think twice about the prospect of a second marriage and/or divorce.

These are very thought provoking facts. Any citizen of the United States must pause when considering the awesome consequences of government action on our society.

214

The Ray of Hope

Now let us review the concept of "How" Americans go offshore. It is clearly through the USE of foreign based entities. It is essential to the success of the concept that the United States citizen learn to accept that this is a tried and tested system that has been in place for years. It has been used by wealthy individuals for hundreds of years and is now becoming more readily available to middle income individuals.

The rules of the United States tax system have created the need to give particular care in the creation and administration of the structure. If we are to legally avoid tax on the profit of the company or trust, we must accept the fact that all connecting factors to the United States citizen or company must be broken.

You do not need millions of dollars to make this work. You can begin by a simple inexpensive IBC as outlined below and transfer as little as $50,000 in after tax liquid assets. This will translate to an impressive retirement plan over time and can be added to at any time. Investments can be made that are conservative and safe. Many foreign based mutual funds are showing a consistent 15% to 25% growth. We are convinced that offshore structures will be the acceptable IRA of the 90's. So, if the company or trust is operated properly this is all tax free.

The rest of the world is very aware of the changes in United States policy. As we have stated earlier in the book, we are the only country that does some of these things and we are the only country that taxes our residents and citizens, business or personal, in whatever jurisdiction they choose to reside.

The International Tax Planners Association is a group of over a thousand lawyers, accountants, bank officers, trust officers, and business advisors who work full time to build systems that will create the best possible results for their clients. Over 90% of the members are foreign based. Many of these clients are United States citizens or are individuals of great wealth who are planning to emigrate to the United States and need to do something to separate themselves from their assets before they take up residence here. This takes careful planning, but once done the techniques are available for other uses.

Members of the ITPA have been acting in this capacity for years. This is not new to them and the company and trust systems that are developed worldwide are in a large part directed at the United States because of its strange relationship to the citizen taxpayer.

In the last several years, most of the meetings and workshops that are held by this group and those of the Offshore Institute have been directed toward methods of Asset Protection for Americans. It is the result of the massive increase in interest by Americans in these sorts of structures. Tax havens of the past have redirected their emphasis from tax relief to asset protection. Many of the sixty (60) "tax havens" of the world are looking at changes in their laws to satisfy this growing awareness by Americans and this need that is evident. There is an incredible pent up demand that is in the process of release.

Do not think this is going un-noticed. Three years ago the British Virgin Islands changed their laws to allow a very private and useful entity called an International Business Corporation, an IBC. Other jurisdictions throughout the Caribbean have followed their lead and created a similar structure that is both private and useful for protection of assets, as well as reduction in tax exposure.

At the last count the BVI had registered over 108,000 IBC's, mostly from middle class Americans that sought relief. The Bahamas are one of the countries that followed suit, along with certain well-known countries like the Turks and Caicos Islands and the Cayman Islands. The Bahamas have registered over 90,000 IBC's in the last two years. It is a very competitive business and these countries know that they must produce a product that will provide privacy, protection and profit potential to survive as a viable offshore business and financial center.

The Isle of Man hybrid company we have written about in this book is considered by the experts as the Cadillac of Business structures offering asset protection. Many times a person of substantial wealth will choose the best that money can buy.

However with the growth of the Caribbean IBC's there is an alternative that is considerably less expensive to create and to maintain. Two years ago Intercon Associates opened an office in the Cayman Islands to handle the increase in demand for the Caribbean alternative. We had chosen first to satisfy that need by making the Caribbean IBC a subsidiary of the Isle of Man company. Time and experience have taught us that we can now move more aggressively to this structure, as the first unit, if it is properly created and the holder of beneficial interest is not the client.

The principals of Intercon Associates have over 15 years experience in offshore strategic planning and are well recognized in the world business community as a company that will not take chances in creation of a structure that might not withstand the scrutiny of the government or the plaintiff's attorney. For all these years we have held that to do this properly we must be personally and intimately involved in the plan.

A Great Business Opportunity

With the last election and the increase in interest in international tax planning we have had to look for ways to duplicate our services and to train other competent business advisors in the use of offshore planning. To that end we have created a new consults group that will be available to business and trust advisors, attorneys and accountants, to assist them in the launch of a new aspect of their business.

We will sell regional consultants a highly organized three month consultancy contract that will outline in detail all the systems we use. We also recognize that our most valuable commodity is the network of world wide contact we have developed over the last ten years. As part of this consultation, we will take the consultant to the tax haven of his choice and personally introduce him or her to the people who will be most responsible for his offshore success.

Additionally, as part of the consultation, we will come to the region in which the consultant will work and will hold an asset protection seminar on his behalf to launch him or her in this very profitable endeavor. Each of us is an experienced speaker and has lectured on business structures and international tax planning in various countries around the world.

The principles of this new group are as follows:

Dr. Larry Turpen, the author of this book, President of LAD Financial Services in Reno, Nevada and originator of the Intercon Group of Companies based in Europe and the Caribbean is the chairman of the group of affiliated companies that will train the contracted consultants. He has over 30 years experience in offshore planning and has headed, or served as chief consultant to the companies listed above for the last 8 years. His training includes the Graduate

218

School of Business at the University of California, Berkeley as well as graduate courses at Oxford University in England.

Mr. Jim Harris, formally President of Corporate Service Center in Reno, Nevada, which he recently sold to spend full time in his new venture, Corporate Consultants, Inc. This company will be the source of all domestic entities, such as corporations, trusts, limited liability companies, and limited partnerships. His experience in this field will be an essential element to train our group of consultants in the United States.

LAD Financial Services itself will be expanded to include serving as the corporate office center for domestic entities that need a staffed office arrangement in the State of Nevada. This includes those individuals that select Nevada for its zero percent tax rate on companies and for the domicile of the domestic structure when they live or work in another state. By having a proper office in Nevada the tax bite can be reduced significantly.

Finally, we are affiliated with the Law Firm of James E. Burk of Washington, D. C. This allows us to have every document that is produced by our affiliated organization to be reviewed by a qualified attorney. By so doing, this gives the purchaser a sense of security in the propriety of the documentation, from an American point of view.

Intercon Associates board of directors has determined that there are over a hundred population centers in the United States that could better serve clients needing this kind of service. If we organized a group of service providers and offered these individuals or companies a consultancy contract that would train them in the marketing and servicing of the offshore planning techniques, as outlined in this book, this ned would be met.

It is felt that the best service can be provided on a personal basis. A group of qualified individuals who have purchased a territorial right to service clients in a select geographical area would both enhance the quality of service and the availability of IBC's and foreign trusts to a larger audience.

A complete business plan has been created that will allow the prospective consultant to see how this addition to his product or service line will enhance his income. The five year proforma shows an incredible alternate income source from the sale of this service. This plan is available upon request.

So, there you have it! The addition of the product or service of an offshore company or international business corporation is essential to your financial well being. They are readily available and our group of consultants nationwide will be able to provide that service at a high level of competence.

In the back of this book is detailed information for contacting LAD Financial Services for any of the following reasons.

- If you are interested in a private consultation we would be happy to arrange one.

- If you would simply like to begin and want the input forms necessary to form a company for your use along with a fee schedule. This would be followed by personal contact from a qualified consultant.

- If you are interested in becoming qualified as a consultant and are interested in the business plan and the income that can be earned satisfying the demand for this service in your area. We will be happy to arrange an appointment where you can come and meet with us to discuss this possibility.

We will discuss with you the three month consultation with our experts and the ongoing consultancy service you can have access to as you build your business.

We can be contacted through:

LAD Financial Service, Inc.
1005 Terminal Way, #110
Reno, NV 89502

Notes:

Maps

225

Appendix I
The Isle of Man:
A Business and Tax
Haven

Geography

The Isle of Man is located in the northern part of the Irish Sea, equidistant from Ireland, Scotland, and England at the center of the British Isles. It is 227 square miles in size, about half of which is mountainous. The highest point is the summit of Snaefell, 2,036 feet.

The name of the island is derived from uncertain Celtic origins. The ancient Celtic name was Manna, whose derivative form "Mannin" is the modern Manx Gaelic name. This was Latinized in the Dark Ages as Mannia. Hence the old and correct English name spelled "Mann," or as it is usually spelled today, "Man" or "Isle of Man." Its people are called "Manx." The word derives from the Norse "Manxk," anglicized as Manks, or Manx.

Constitution and History

Historically and culturally, the Isle of Man and its native people belong to the Gaelic world incorporating Ireland and West Scotland. In the 9th century, the Vikings from Scandinavia conquered the Hebrides and the Isle of Man and set up the kingdom of the Sudreys. After four centuries, the kingdom broke up, but Man remained as the heir of the old kingdom and, despite varying fortunes through the following centuries, the Isle of Man remains as the last remnant of that ancient kingdom.

Consequently, the Isle of Man is not and never has been fully incorporated into Ireland, Scotland, Wales, or England, and is not and never has been a part of the United Kingdom. The infrastructure of the Manx government, law church, and tradition remains clearly derived from the Gaelic-Norse kingdom that ended in the 14th century.

Today the British monarch is also the Lord of Mann (the title of king was dropped in the Middle Ages), and although there are strong and close links between the British and Manx governments, the Isle of Man remains autonomous, self-governing, and financially self-reliant.

The legislative body in Man is known as the Tynwald and is divided into two houses. The lower house, the House of Keys, is directly elected by the people. The upper house, the Legislative Council, formerly consisted of officers of state, but is now indirectly elected from the House of Keys. The British monarch is represented by a Lieutenant-Governor.

The Tynwald celebrated its millennium (1,000 years) in 1979, making it the oldest continuous democracy in the world today.

The executive power is in the hands of the Chief Minister, elected by the Tynwald. Below that position are seven ministers, each heading up a department of government. Other members of the Tynwald also serve as junior ministers in departments of government. The Chief Minister and the other ministers make up the Executive Council, which acts as the supreme executive body, and which advises the Lieutenant-Governor.

The judiciary is composed of two Deemsters (high court judges) and subordinate magistrates. The Manx legal profession is separate and distinct from its counterparts in the remainder of the British Isles. Manx law was originally based on the island's own customary law, but English common law has, over the centuries, been absorbed into Manx law. In many respects, particularly in commercial law, Manx law is similar to the laws of England.

International Relations

Although the Isle of Man has self-government and issues its own passports, in matters of international law the United Kingdom is responsible for Manx affairs. However, in relation to the Common Market, the Isle of Man enjoys a peculiar status. In terms of Protocol 3 of the Treaty of Accession of the United Kingdom, the Isle of Man is not a member of the European Community, but is treated as if it were a member for all purposes of tariffs, trade, and freedom of movement of goods and capital. Its independent status is thus affirmed by the European Community.

Customs Union

There is a customs agreement between the Isle of Man and the United Kingdom. Apart from a few exceptions, customs, excise duties, and value-added tax (VAT) are maintained at the same rates as in the U.K. However, the Manx Customs and Excise Service are entirely separate from its British counterpart.

Communications

Air

Ronaldsway Airport is located in the south of the island and some 9 miles from the capital, Douglas. Services are scheduled all-year-round and are maintained to and from Dublin and Belfast in Ireland, and from Glasgow, Blackpool, Liverpool, and Manchester. Jet service is offered from London's Heathrow airport. In the summer, additional flights are added to other locations in Britain. Air taxis are also available.

Sea

The Isle of Man Steam Packet Company Limited operates roll-on and roll-off ferries to Britain and Ireland. A year-round service is maintained to Heysham, England. In the summer, this is extended to cover Belfast, Dublin, Stranraer, Fleetwood, and Liverpool.

Postal

The Manx Postal Authority is a government department, quite separate from its British or Irish counterparts, issuing its own stamps.

Telecommunications

Telephone and telex services are administered by Manx Telecom, a subsidiary of British Telecommunications. A full range of international services is available, including direct-dialing facilities to most countries of the world.

Radio and Television

Apart from the local station, Manx Radio, all of the principal British and Irish stations can be heard. There is no local television, but BBC and ITV channels from Britain cover the island. On the west side of the island, Irish television can be received.

230

The People

The Manx people are English-speaking, although the visitor will see signs in Manx Gaelic and may occasionally hear it spoken. The professional classes usually have received higher education in Britain, and as a result most of the people visiting business people will meet will have a close familiarity with the British and international scene. In addition, of course, there are a considerable number of people of non-Manx origin living on the island. Most of these have come from Britain or Ireland. The population is approximately 75,000.

There is long tradition of hospitality in the Isle of Man, and immigrants are absorbed easily and comfortably. The English concept of the "class system" is alien to the Manx people.

The Economy

Traditionally based on tourism, agriculture, and fishing, the economy today is based primarily on international finance and banking, light manufacturing industry, and tourism.

Douglas, the capital, with over half the population is the center of the tourist and finance industry. There are considerable government incentives for new business.

Currency and Banking

The currency of the island is pound sterling. Most notes and coins in circulation are issued by the Manx government, but U.K. notes and coins are also in circulation and are readily accepted by all merchants.

The banking system in the Isle of Man is operationally integrated with the banking system of England. The principal bank is the Isle of Man Bank Limited, which is a subsidiary of National Westminister Bank Plc. It dominates the commercial banking scene and is the banker for the Manx government. However, the Manx banking system is legally separate from the banking system of the United Kingdom, and information held by Manx banks is not available to the U.K. authorities unless it relates to a proven case of criminal activity.

There are many banks operating on the Isle of Man. It is estimated that all of the major banks in Britain and the continent of Europe are represented on the isle, as well as many banks from North America. The Manx banking industry is controlled by legislation and a government license is necessary before commencing operations. Banks are closely supervised by the Financial Services Commission. In matters of negotiable instruments, bills of exchange, or cheques, Manx law is identical to those of England.

Ship Registration

The Isle of Man has comprehensive ship registration facilities coupled with international recognition. Shipping registration and management is a fast-growing industry on the Isle of Man.

Insurance

The insurance industry is closely linked with the insurance industry of England. However, as with banks, Manx insurance companies are licensed and supervised by the Insurance Supervision Commission. Insurance companies offer products that are a safe form of asset protection in that no creditor can have access to any asset held under an insurance product. There is a flourishing captive insurance industry based on the island as well.

Companies and Trusts

The law on Manx companies and trusts is broadly similar to that of England and Ireland. Because of the flexibility of Manx law, Manx companies and trusts are widely used internationally.

The island contains the home office of many worldwide companies administrative offices and offers these services to clients internationally.

There are many investment management institutions and related institutions in the Isle of Man. Such companies, as with banks, are regulated and supervised by the Financial Supervision Commission.

Immigration and Land Ownership

At present, there are no restrictions on immigration or land ownership, apart from those resulting from a common citizenship with the United Kingdom. However, it is by no means certain this situation will continue indefinitely. Many business people who establish business entities on the island will find it advantageous to live in Ireland, Scotland, or England and thereby retain the non-resident status of the company formation.

Work permits are required by all who do not qualify as Manx patronals or Isle of Man workers, or who do not have specific exemption.

Government Policy

While the Manx government tends to be conservative, there is no political party system. However, combined with conservatism there is a strong sense of Manx national identity.

Relations with the United Kingdom and the Republic of Ireland are cordial and, while the Manx government is eager to promote the well-being of the Manx economy, it is most unlikely to promote any activity that could harm relations with either neighbor.

The Manx government is enthusiastic in the promotion of international finance activities and in the promotion of manufacturing industry. It has established a free port facility in the island and has determined upon a policy to increase the population of the island by attracting suitable immigrants.

A Brief Guide to Manx Taxation

Independence

The Isle of Man, being independent and self-governing, has its own taxation system completely independent of the taxation system of the United Kingdom. It is independent not merely in the context of its administration, but also in that its relations with the U.K. Inland Revenue is no different from its relations with any other foreign tax authority. There is no flow of information between the Manx and British tax bodies other than that provided for in the normal way under the Double Taxation Treaty. The Assessor of Income Tax is the government official responsible for the assessment of tax. The Treasury of the Manx government is the collecting body.

Direct Taxation

The only direct taxation is income tax at a standard rate of 20%. This tax applies to individuals and resident companies. However, for the tax year 1988-89, the rate of income tax on the first £6,000 of taxable income is at the lower rate of 15% for individuals.

For resident companies, dividends are treated as a charge against profits before arriving at taxable profit. There is no capital gains tax, estate duty, wealth tax, surtax, or gift tax. Income tax is assessable on the worldwide income of Manx residents. In the context of companies, however, there are many Manx-incorporated but non-resident companies, and these are not liable to Manx income tax. Investment holding and dealing companies, and shipping companies whose income is derived from outside the island and which are beneficially owned outside the island, can obtain exemption from Manx income tax.

Insurance companies carrying on business in the Isle of Man are subject to normal tax on underwriting and investment profits. However, insurance companies licensed under the Exempt Insurance Companies Act 1981 are totally exempt from income tax.

Investment trust companies, which meet certain criteria relating to their international activities, may also obtain exemption from withholding tax. This is accomplished by distributing the whole of their profits to shareholders by way of dividends. Under certain circumstances, income of trusts is exempt from taxation.

Residence

A Manx company is non-resident when a majority of its directors reside outside the Isle of Man, and meetings of the directors take place outside the island.

Non-Resident Companies

A Manx-incorporated but non-resident company is exempt from any income taxation in the Isle of Man except in so far as it carries on any trade or business in the Isle of Man. It is liable to non-resident company duty, which is levied at a flat annual rate.

Withholding Tax

A Manx resident company is obliged to deduct withholding tax of 20% from all dividends, interest, or other such payment payable to a non-resident. However, interest on deposits with authorized banks is exempt from withholding tax by extra-statutory concession. This does not apply to exempt insurance companies, to exempt investment trust companies, or to exempt investment and shipping companies.

Double Taxation Treaty

The only double taxation treaty existing is with the United Kingdom. It is an old treaty and, to a large degree, obsolete. There is no intention to negotiate a new treaty.

Trusts

A Manx resident trust is assessable like any other Manx resident. However, by special concession there is no tax on trusts where the beneficiaries are non-resident, and where the funds in the trust are derived from non-resident sources and remain invested outside the Isle of Man or are deposited with those banks approved for the purposes of the concession mentioned above (see Withholding Tax, above).

Stamp Duties and Other Indirect Taxation

There is no stamp or capital duties, except in relation to the share capital of companies, purchase and sale of property, and other legal documents. This does not include share transfers, which are free of stamp duty.

A Brief Guide to Manx Company Law

The Law

The Isle of Man has a legal system based on common law. At present, the principal companies act is the Companies Consolidation Act 1931, although there has been subsequent amending legislation, with the most recent in 1986. The Isle of Man Companies Act 1931 is based on the U.K. Companies Act 1929. The following types of company can be formed.

1. Companies Limited by Shares, private or public.
2. Companies Unlimited with Shares, private or public.
3. Companies Limited by Guarantee, private or public.
4. Companies Limited by Guarantee and having shares, private or public.

In addition, under the Partnership Act 1909, limited partnerships can be formed in the Isle of Man. Private companies are formed with two subscribers, by a simple registration process. The constitution of a company is defined in the "Memorandum and Articles of Association." Public companies are more complex. Since the majority of offshore companies are private, we shall not further consider public companies.

Memorandum of Association: The Memorandum sets out the name and capital structure of the company. Since 1988, there has been no need to state "objects."

Articles of Association: The Articles of Association provide the internal regulations of the company. The articles can be drawn up to suit the individual requirements of each company, but there are certain specified requirements.

As a guide, there are specimen (but not obligatory) forms of Articles of Association published as regulations by the Treasury. Basically, the affairs of the company are run by the directors, who comprise the board of the company. Articles can be amended by special resolution.

Names: There are certain restrictions on the use of names. In particular, names containing the words "Bank" or "Banking," "Trust," "Building Society," "Municipal," "Chartered," "Royal," "Co-operative," "International," and "Isle of Man" are likely to come under scrutiny. The registrar of companies can and does review a name and has the power to require an existing name be changed. Names are reviewed on application and unacceptable names are rejected.

Members and Shareholders: The minimum number of members permissible in a company is two. There is no maximum. If at any time the number of members in a limited liability company falls below two, the remaining member becomes liable without limit for the company's debts. A private company may not invite the public to subscribe for its shares or debentures.

Where a company limited by shares wishes to reduce its share capital, this is done by special resolution at an extraordinary general meeting. Such resolution has to be confirmed by the courts before taking effect. An unlimited company may reduce its capital by special resolution without reference to the courts.

A company with shares may have different classes of shares, with different rights and obligations attaching to each class. A company limited by guarantee does not issue shares, but may have different classes of members.

Officers: Every company must have at least two directors and a secretary. It may have alternate directors, and an assistant secretary in addition.

Debentures: Companies may issue debentures. As is the case in other common law jurisdictions, debentures secured by a floating charge can be issued by a company.

Registration of Charges: Certain charges against the assets of a company must be registered with the registrar of companies. These include: floating charges, property mortgages, charges on book debts, ships, and a few other minor charges.

Legal Formalities: The registered office of the company must be notified to the registrar of companies. At the office, a notice must be displayed in a conspicuous position, stating the name of the company. The company must have a seal, which is normally kept at its registered office. Duplicate seals can be kept abroad. The company must maintain records of:

1. Minutes of directors' and members meetings.

2. Register of members.

3. Register of charges.

4. Proper accounts and records.

The company's accounts are not filed at the registry but audited accounts must be presented to the members annually. The auditors need not be Manx residents. The company's letters must have its name, registered office, place and number of incorporation, and names (and nationality, if not British) of directors printed on the letterhead.

Returns: Returns must be made to the registrar of companies of:

1. Allotments etc., of shares.

2. Directors and secretaries.

3. Registered office.

The annual return lists the names of registered share-holders. These may be nominees. In the case of a Company Limited by Guarantee, and a Company Limited by Guarantee and having shares, the return does not include the names of members.

Bearer Share Companies: Both public and private companies may issue their shares in bearer form.

Manx Exempt Insurance Companies

The Insurance Act 1986: This act prohibits any company from carrying on an insurance business in the Isle of Man unless it is duly licensed by the Manx government. The act sets out the licensing and regulatory framework for insurance companies.

Exempt Insurance Companies Act 1981: Under the Exempt Insurance Companies Act 1981, the government has the power to exempt totally from Manx income tax any insurance company, the whole of whose underwriting risks is located outside the Isle of Man.

Exempt Insurance Companies Rules 1981: These provide that, to qualify under the Exempt Insurance Companies Act 1981 for exemption from income tax, the following provisions will apply:

1. The share capital should normally be not less than £50,000, fully paid in cash.

2. A solvency margin must be maintained of not less than 15% of the premiums written in the previous year.

3. Management accounts must be submitted to the government quarterly, and audited accounts must be submitted annually.

4. The directors and management of the company must

be acceptable to the government. Not less than half of the directors must be Manx-resident.

5. The re-insurance arrangements must be submitted to and be acceptable to the government.

6. An initial license fee of £2,000 will be payable.

Taxation: Insurance companies underwriting risks in the Isle of Man are liable to normal Manx income taxation on underwriting and investment profits in the usual way. However, insurance companies exempted under the Exempt Insurance Companies Act 1981 are totally exempt from tax on all their profits.

Exemptions from Withholding Tax

As already noted, a withholding tax of 20% (officially called "non-resident income tax") is applied to payments of dividends, royalties, rents, etc., received by Manx resident companies to non-residents. This does not apply to non-resident Manx companies, which are not liable to Manx income tax. Since dividends paid by a company are allowed as a charge against the company's profits before tax, dividends are paid out of the pre-tax profits, and thus there is no double taxation.

The following exceptions and exemptions from withholding tax are of significance:

1. Bank Interest: Interest paid by banks is paid gross, without any deduction of tax, both to residents and non-residents.

2. Investment Trust Companies: Dividends paid by exempted investment trusts to non-residents are exempted from withholding tax. Thus, where such a company distributes all its income, there is no Manx income tax.

3. Trusts: Income payable to non-resident beneficiaries is free of Manx income or withholding taxes where the income is derived from outside the island, and all the income beneficiaries are non-resident.

4. Investment Dealing Companies: Exempted investment holding or dealing companies investments including securities, commodities, and property are exempt from all Manx income tax. There is a flat annual fee payable. No withholding tax is applied.

5. Shipping Companies: Exempted shipping companies are exempt from all Manx income tax. As with the above companies, there is a flat annual fee payable. Such companies must be resident in the Isle of Man, and carry on business in the Isle of Man. Ships will be registered under the Manx flag, and comply with Manx shipping legislation. This legislation requires standards of safety and crewing identical with those of the United Kingdom.

Exempt Trusts

A trust with a Manx resident trustee is subject to Manx taxation, like any other Manx resident, at the rate of 20% on income. However, by special concession, such a trust will not be assessed to Manx tax when it:

1. Is funded from sources outside the Isle of Man.

2. Has no income arising in the Isle of Man (other than bank interest).

3. Has its beneficiaries resident outside the Isle of Man.

The taxation position of a Manx trust in relation to other countries' tax law is complex, and different considerations apply in each country.

Underlying Companies

Because of its nature, a trust does not normally trade, although it can hold investments, and thereby form and own companies. It is thus usually simpler for the assets of a trust to be vested in holding or trading companies wholly owned by the trust.

This structure has many other advantages in the context of administration. A single holding company can be owned by more than one trust, thus preserving the ownership of shares in an enterprise in one name, but effectively allocating the ownership to different individuals in defined proportions. Such a holding company can be exempt from Manx income tax under the Income Tax (Exempt Companies) Act 1984, where the trust or trusts are exempt.

Unit Trusts

This tax exemption applies equally to unit trusts or mutual funds, where a deed of trust forms the constitution of the fund.

Non-Resident Companies

Residence:

As noted earlier, the definition of a company residence for purposes of Manx income tax is of great importance. A company is deemed resident in the Isle of Man if a majority of its directors are personally resident, and if the meetings of the directors take place in the Isle of Man. A company a majority of whose directors are resident outside the Isle of Man is considered non-resident.

A non-resident company is considered, in spite of being incorporated under Manx law, to be an overseas company, and is taxable in the Isle of Man only in so far as it trades or has income arising in the Isle of Man. If it receives dividends from a Manx-resident company, withholding tax is applied to the dividend.

The question of where a non-resident company actually is resident is largely academic. Many jurisdictions in Europe and overseas, including the United States, do not have this concept of residence. So, a Manx company with directors in the United States, and holding its meetings there, would only be liable to U.S. tax if it carried on business in, or had income arising in the United States.

Non-Liability to Tax

Thus, a Manx non-resident company can provide an effective tax-exempt vehicle. By doing so it is exposed to attack by U.S. revenue authorities by virtue of its "floating" state of residence. Such companies pay a flat annual fee in the Isle of Man through non-resident company duty. Many times this is done through the use of management companies who assume the responsibility for paying annual fees and keeping the company in good standing.

Overseas Companies

Registration: Companies formed outside the Isle of Man, but carrying on business in the Isle of Man, are obliged to register themselves in the Manx company register as such. However, when such a company is managed from the Isle of Man, but carries on no business in the Isle of Man, there is no requirement to register.

Taxation: The concepts set out in Section 6 (non-resident companies) apply equally to non-Manx companies. Technically, where such companies have their directors residing in and the board meetings held in the Isle of Man, they are liable to Manx income tax. However, such companies can have their directors overseas, but be administered from the Isle of Man, without any Manx tax liability at all. However, this gives rise to an exposure to attack by U.S. Revenue authorities by virtue of its "floating"' state of residence.

Exemption: Under the Income Tax (Exempt Companies) Act 1984, such companies, when carrying on the business of holding or dealing in investments, or managing ships, can be resident in the Isle of Man, but exempt from income tax altogether.

The Income Tax (Exempt Companies) Act of 1984: Summary

The act received the Royal Assent in June 1984. This section explains its provisions.

(a) Clause 1. The act applies to:

(i) Manx incorporated companies and (ii) Companies incorporated outside the Isle of Man, but registered in the Isle of Man as foreign companies carrying on business in the Isle of Man, where such companies are carrying on business in:

(i) Investment and commodity holding and dealing (investments includes property, patent rights, royalties, and similar rights).

(ii) Management of ships overseas.

(b) Clause 2 (1). Such companies can be exempted from Manx income tax if:

(i) All the income or receipts derive from activities outside the Isle of Man.

(ii) No person in the Isle of Man has any beneficial interest in such company (except where such interest arises through a shareholding in a public company whose shares are quoted on a recognized stock exchange).

(c) Clause 2 (2). The following activities would not constitute trading in the Isle of Man.

(i) Holding Manx government securities.

(ii) Maintaining bank accounts in the Isle of Man.

(iii) Managing the company and its trading activities in the Isle of Man.

(d) Clauses 2 (4) and 2 (5). An exempt company must have:

(i) One director, at least, resident in the Isle of Man.

(ii) The secretary, (who shall be an individual) resident in the Isle of Man. The secretary must be professionally qualified, or be approved by the Manx government.

(e) Clauses 3 (1) and 3 (2). The Manx "year of assessment" runs from April 6 to the following April 5. To obtain exemption for a year of assessment, the application should be submitted before June 30, or within 30 days of commencing business. A fee is payable at the time of company organization. A late application can be made up to September 30, but the fee for a late application is £1,000. To renew the application in subsequent years, the Manx director must submit a statutory declaration prior to June 30.

(f) Clauses 3 (3) to Clause 5. If the conditions set out at (b) above are broken, the assessor has discretion either to set aside the exemptions, or if the breach is minor, to disregard it. There is a right of appeal for a company, whose exemption has been set aside, to the income tax commissioners. The income tax commissioners, in such circumstances, may require the disclosure to them of the identity of the beneficial owner, but such information is totally confidential to them.

(g) Clause 6. An exempt company is exempt from any withholding tax.

(h) Clause 7. Exemption may be voluntarily surrendered.

(i) Clause 12. If such a company employs staff directly in the Isle of Man, it must still deduct tax from the salaries of its employees.

The Use of Exempt Investment Companies

We set out below a number of key considerations when contemplating the use of such companies.

1. Freedom from Manx tax. This is useful when income is received gross from jurisdictions without withholding taxes, or, for example, U.K. exempt gifts.

2. Anonymity. The beneficial ownership is effectively concealed.

3. Residence. A company can be Manx-resident legally and officially, without giving rise to Manx taxation. This is particularly attractive for Liberian, Panamanian, and other companies that otherwise tend to float in a no-man's land. For example, a Panamanian company can have directors in Monaco, but cannot trade from there. Such a company could carry out all its functions in the Isle of Man.

4. Cost. The Isle of Man is, in any event, one of the cheaper jurisdictions in the world for offshore companies. By using the provisions of this legislation, the extra expense of overseas directors can be avoided, and the administration made more cost-effective.

247

The Use of Exempt Shipping Companies

The comments above are applicable. A few further comments would be useful in the light of Manx shipping legislation.

1. Ships can be entered on the Manx Register of Shipping and fly either the U.K. Red Ensign or the Manx Red Ensign (the same as the U.K. flag but with the Manx symbol of "three legs" on the right-hand side).

2. Such ships must be owned by a Manx-incorporated and resident company (although under the Exempt Companies (Income Tax) Act 1984, they may be exempt from Manx tax).

3. Such ships must comply with safety regulations which are identical to those of the United Kingdom.

4. Such ships must conform to officer and crewing regulations which are identical to those of the United Kingdom.

The advantage, therefore, is solely in the context of exemption from taxation, etc., and an effective and sympathetic base for management of the shipping company.

Isle of Man Guarantee Companies

Origins: The origins of "Companies Limited by Guarantee," and "Companies Limited by Guarantee and having shares" (which we call hybrid companies because of their mixed type of capital), lie in English common law. The first Companies Acts in England were essentially building on earlier trust concepts. In civil law jurisdictions, however, a rather more radical approach produced not merely different forms of company, but also a different concept of the usage of a company.

In the Isle of Man, company law followed the development of English company law. Indeed, company law in the Isle of Man until 1948 was identical to English company law. The first Companies Act in the Isle of Man was passed in 1865. This was replaced in 1910 by a new Companies Act, and this was, in its turn replaced by the Companies Consolidation Act of 1931, which is still the basic Companies Act in force.

Each of these Manx acts followed a year or two after English company acts. However, in the Isle of Man, the process of following stopped in 1931, although there have been several subsequent amending acts (the latest being in 1982). The 1931 legislation is still however, the primary act.

The Companies Consolidation Act 1931 follows the U.K. Companies Act of 1929 in virtually every respect. It may be noted that almost identical legislation forms the basic companies' legislation of Gibraltar, British Virgin Islands, and many other old dependencies and colonies of the British Empire. The later U.K. Act, in 1948, was never adopted in the Isle of Man, although some dependencies, including Cyprus, did so, and it forms the basic act of those countries.

It is worth noting at this stage that some British dependencies did not follow this pattern. The Channel Islands, for example, with their inheritance of the French tradition, adopted a compromise company law during the last century that has not basically changed, and which provides only for the conventional company limited by shares.

Companies Limited by Guarantee derives from this early period of English company law. Unlike Roman or civil law systems, English law has always endeavored in essence to determine and adopt customary practices rather than impose a "rational" philosophical framework of law. English company law, indeed, evolved from trust law.

Characteristics: Prior to the introduction of limited liability companies, there was no way to limit the liability of members of commercial associations, and such associations were effectively extended partnerships. Partnerships then, as now, could take many forms and shapes that evolved or were deliberately planned with the objectives of each enterprise in mind. As the need for more sophisticated legal definition emerged, so did English company law evolve. Towards the end of the 19th century, the various forms of corporate associations under English law had evolved. These can, simply, be set out as follows:

1. Associations whose members contributed to the capital of the company and acquired rights pro rata to their contribution to the capital. Such rights were called shares. Each member held a "share" of the equity related to their contribution. This is the type of company with which everyone is familiar. A share certificate is issued by the company certifying the "shares" held by each member. Such shares are transferable, (although, in the case of a private company, with restrictions) and the certificates are securities under Exchange Control Regulations.

2. However, often associations did not want to have pro rata definition of member's rights as is implicit in the concept of shares. For example, a social club would not wish to distribute income. Its members would not want to buy their membership, but would be happy to contribute, as members, to its funds. They would

be happy to pay a set entry subscription and a set annual subscription. They would not want transferable memberships.

Yet they also wanted limited liability. So, the law provided a provision for a company to be incorporated, and to be limited by guarantee. In this type of company, no initial capital was paid. Persons could be elected into membership without any cash requirement, although normally each new member was expected to pay an entry subscription upon election to membership at a rate as determined by the directors. However, every member, whether an entry subscription was paid or not, by virtue of election to membership, guaranteed to pay a set sum (determined by the articles of incorporation) upon demand, in the event of the company being insolvent upon its liquidation. A member's liability was limited to their guarantee. Thus we have a company with a member's liability limited to the extent of this guarantee.

Membership ceases on death or resignation. The subscriptions that have been paid (both the initial entry subscriptions as well as any subsequent annual subscriptions) are not returnable upon a member ceasing to be a member. In principle, each member has equal voting rights and equal rights to income or capital distributions, should any be made, although flexibility in these matters can be provided to allow for different classes of membership (e.g., associate membership, non-voting membership, etc.)

3. Finally, the law recognized another variant on the theme of limited liability. Some companies wanted to have a share capital in the ordinary way, and also to provide that members would additionally guarantee a set contribution to liabilities not necessarily in pro-

portion to their capital contributions. If it was a matter of there being a guarantee pro rata with each share, this could be overcome by having part paid shares. Sometimes, it was desired that the guarantee should be the same for each member, irrespective of the amount of shareholding. Further, it was sometimes desired to have a company where some members subscribed the capital in shares, but other members could become members without subscribing for shares, thus providing a flexibility in the context of voting rights, and participation in profits or other privileges.

In modern terms, we can think of a proprietary club along these lines, which has "owning" members, and "customer" members! So, to meet these needs, the Company Limited by Guarantee and having a share capital was devised. However, we are here concerned with Companies Limited by Guarantee, which we will now call guarantee companies, and with Companies Limited by Guarantee and having a share capital, which we will now call hybrid companies. We will therefore ignore conventional share-issuing companies.

Guarantee Companies

We will now examine guarantee companies in their modern context. As noted, wherever English company law is the model company law, guarantee companies can be formed. The universal mandatory provisions specifically affecting guarantee companies are:

1. The articles must state the number of members with which the company is to be registered. This can be increased subsequently, but notice of any increase must be filed with the company registry.

2. If there are more than 50 members, the company will be a public company, and subject to the regulations governing public companies.

3. There must be a minimum number of members: usually 2 or 3 for a private company and 7 for a public company, depending upon the place of incorporation.

4. Such companies are not generally expected to distribute profits. The legislation usually provides for a guarantee company to be capable of distributing profits only to members and for distributions to others to be void. However, the articles of incorporation may provide for the rights to distribution to be separated from membership as such, thereby enabling a member to sell their rights to a third party. An analogy is the beneficiary of a trust selling their rights to trust income to a third party. Unless otherwise determined by the articles, each member participates equally. This is irrespective of any variation in subscriptions paid.

In addition, of course, the normal requirements of company law relating to all companies, whether with share capital or not, apply. These relate to the necessity to hold general meetings, keep minutes and accounts, have accounts audited and presented to the members, and make returns to the company registry. However, it is worth noting that the annual returns of guarantee companies do not include the names of the members. These names are not on the public register and are recorded only in the private records of the company.

Within this framework, there is a great deal of flexibility available in structuring a company to achieve its objectives. It is impossible to cover every eventuality, and so the options set out below are merely a few suggestions to indicate the variations available:

A. Although the company must have at least two directors to control the company, there may also be a protector, as is often found in trusts, and it may be made obligatory for the directors to have his or her consent before implementing defined decisions, such as election of new members, or disposing of company assets.

B. There may be one or more classes of members with differing rights to vote, or participate in income or capital distributions.

C. There may be prohibitions on certain classes of members, or prohibitions on members' resident in certain defined countries from participating in income distributions, or from holding other rights.

D. With regard to the transferability of membership, there is no doubt that membership is an "interest" in a company. A member may transfer his or her interest while remaining a member. Although, a member may cease to be a member by resignation or death, the "interest" remains. While this can cause problems, it may also create opportunities for tax planning. Of course, the articles of incorporation can specifically state that upon the death or resignation of a member, their "interest" ceases. This would then be analogous to the position of a life interest in a trust.

Often a member will wish to provide for his or her death by nominating a successor to be elected a member. The member can do this in several ways. Sometimes, the articles of incorporation may stipulate that an heir, who will have an "interest," must be elected a member. Or the member can give the directors a letter of wishes, as he or she would to the trustees of a discretionary trust where he is the settler.

Sometimes there can be built into the articles a power

for a member to nominate a successor, who will be deemed to have applied for membership upon the cessation of membership (for whatever reason) of the original member. Such application still has to be approved by the board (which can always refuse it) but election of members in such circumstances may be effected with exemption from entry subscription for the new nominated member.

E. Because membership can be obtained and lost without financial consideration, it can be difficult to put a value upon membership. In this respect it is similar to the status of a beneficiary of a discretionary settlement, but of course a guarantee company is not a trust, and cannot be treated as such.

F. There is an exchange control aspect of guarantee companies. Although a member can be issued with a membership certificate, this does not constitute a share, or stock or security. Consequently, where exchange control regulations refer to securities, these regulations do not affect members of guarantee companies. Nor do requirements for the deposit of securities under Exchange Control Regulations include membership certificates of guarantee companies.

Hybrid Companies

We turn now briefly to hybrid companies. All that has been said about guarantee companies is equally applicable to hybrid companies. However, hybrid companies can provide for the shareholders to be a different group of people than the non-shareholder members. Thus the shareholders could be professional trust administrators, in whom could be vested all the voting and administrative powers, while the beneficial owners could be the non-shareholder members, in whom would be vested all the rights to income and capital. By these means we have divorced control from beneficial interests.

Because the directors and shareholders in hybrid companies can have a great deal of power (for example, to elect further members, and determine income or capital distributions), it is desirable to build into the Articles of Association provisions for the appointment of a protector, whose approval must be obtained for the election of members and disposal of assets. The protector should, of course, be an independent third party, with a relationship with the beneficial owners, so that he or she can both protect their interests and advise the directors when so requested.

We may add also that it is no longer possible to form hybrids in England. The Companies Act 1980 abolished them. We have noted that these companies provide variable degrees of member control. We have in these vehicles a range of trusts, wrapped up in corporate form, in which the beneficiaries may, or may not, exercise real control.

Aspects of United Kingdom Taxation

Turning now to the use of such companies in legal tax avoidance, we may note that in U.K. law, they are companies and not trusts, and thus the injection of assets into such an entity may give rise to a Section 478 problem, but not an inheritance tax problem. In the context of a U.K. person emigrating to the United States, this can be a great advantage, since the U.S. authorities could, if the company is structured correctly, deem it to be a trust, notwithstanding its corporate form. Thus the emigrant successfully avoids their inheritance tax and controls their U.S. tax liability.

There are two areas of U.K. tax difficulties. In the first, there is little doubt that, if such companies are used blatantly, there is a risk of Section 478 being brought into play. In regard to inheritance tax when a member dies, and their progeny is then elected to membership, it seems to us, in the present climate of tax law, that there has been an effective transfer for inheritance tax purposes, unless the corporate structure has been carefully planned to avoid this. However, there is no case law, and any changes here could have profound effect on the viability of the hundreds of Rugby Clubs, Old Folks Associations, and London Clubs that all use this form of association. Because of the difficulty in valuing "interests," it is difficult to see on what basis the capital gains tax could be applied.

We do not intend to discuss the impact of U.K. tax on offshore guarantee companies to any further extent. We have already noted that there is difficulty in meeting the capital gains tax valuation provisions. We have also noted that inheritance tax does not arise when assets are transferred into the company. However, the situation that may arise when a member dies, and there is an effective transfer of the deceased's interests to the remaining members, is a subject in itself, which still requires further research and consideration.

Aspects of U.S. Taxation

The IRS does not look purely at the form of a structure when determining the basis of its taxation. A trading trust could be taxed as a corporation. Also, a corporation could be taxed as a trust in certain circumstances. We have already noted that where a U.K. person emigrates to the United States, the establishment of a guarantee company to hold their assets prior to arrival in the United States are not a taxable event under U.K. inheritance tax.

But if the IRS treats the corporation as a constructive trust, the beneficial owner would be treated as a beneficiary of a foreign trust established prior to arrival in the United States, and thus the emigrant would not be liable to tax on the income of the trust, unless it is remitted to him or her in the United States. On what basis, therefore, would the IRS determine the tax status of a guarantee company?

First, we note that there is no case law, nor any letter rulings in the United States relating to guarantee or hybrid companies. However, there is material relating to Liechtenstein anstalts, and it is a reasonable assumption that the IRS would approach the problem of guarantee and hybrid companies on a similar basis. Examination of this material does not suggest any set pattern or uniform approach. Rather, the IRS takes a pragmatic approach, based on the facts, and how they meet the IRS criteria for the basis of taxation. In other words, because a vehicle is a company or a trust in law, it is not necessarily taxed as such. In determining the basis of taxation, there are certain criteria.

These criteria are:

1. The existence of associates. (i.e. a number of persons joined together to the enterprise.)

2. An objective to carry on business, and divide the gains and profits thereon.

3. The continuity of the life of the entity.

4. The degree of centralization of management.

5. Whether there is limited liability for the debts of the entity.

The important thing to determine at the outset is whether we want the guarantee company to be taxed as a trust or a company, and then to structure it accordingly to meet fewer or more of the criteria.

To establish the company as a trust for tax purposes, we should be able to defeat three of the five criteria, and with a bit of effort, four out of five. To establish the company as a company for tax purposes, we should have little difficulty in meeting the criteria.

Let us assume that the IRS agrees that a guarantee company is to be taxed as a corporation. This then means that we have to consider the impact of the IRS code on overseas corporations.

First we may note that the guarantee company has no stock or shares. Since the reporting requirements of the IRS code are invariably defined by reference to stock or voting stock, we have to ascertain whether a certificate of membership in a guarantee company can be construed as stock, and whether there is a difference depending on whether the membership carries voting rights or not. This is of importance, as the IRS imposes reporting requirements on U.S. residents where they are participants in foreign companies in certain circumstances. It is crucial, therefore, that these circumstances are examined, relative to companies limited by guarantee.

We may note that, in Sections 957 and 958 of Sub-Part F of the IRS code, in the section relating to Controlled Foreign Corporations, the term Controlled Foreign Corporation is defined as "...any foreign corporation of which more than 50% of the total combined voting power of all classes of stock entitled to vote is owned (within the meaning of Clause 958(a), or is considered as owned by applying the rules of ownership of Section 958(b), by United States shareholders on any day during the taxable year of such foreign corporations."

Section 958(a) tells us that the ownership is not merely a direct holding, but also indirect, and that where such indirect holding is held in conjunction with others, the proportion of such indirectly held stock will be classed as "owned" in this context. However, in Clause 958(a)(3), a special mention is made of foreign mutual insurance companies, where the term "stock" shall include any certificate entitling the holder to voting power in the corporation.

In the context of these guarantee companies, where the member has no stock, but voting power, it would seem reasonable to assume that the IRS may well place an interpretation on the nature of such membership by reference to the voting power, rather than the nature of the participation. On this basis, we must structure the membership as we would for a share-issuing company. Alternatively, we can use a hybrid company, with alien shareholders and U.S. guarantor members. But this then runs us into another problem. If there are two classes of members (as can be done with hybrid companies), being voting shareholder members and non-voting, we will weaken the argument against the guarantee company being taxed as a corporation. In those circumstances, it may be taxed as a trust, with the shareholders being considered as trustees and the non-shareholding members treated as beneficiaries.

Looking now at the rules on personal holding companies and foreign personal holding companies, we note that in Section 532 and 533 of the IRS code, there is imposition of tax on the accumulated and non-distributed income of a U.S. personal holding company, where such accumulation is designed to reduce the tax of the shareholders. This is similar to the U.K. provisions on distributions by closely held companies.

Section 542 defines a personal holding company as having at least 60% of its income as personal holding company income, and that at any time during the last half of the taxable year, more than 50% in value of its outstanding stock is owned, directly or indirectly, by or for not more than five (5) individuals.

Again, there are provisions for attribution of indirectly held stock held in common with others. Again we come up against the word "stock." A guarantee company issues no stock. Since membership of a guarantee company is difficult to value, can there be any reporting requirements?

We may note that personal holding company income is basically passive income, such as dividends, interest, royalties, annuities, rents, and fees from personal service contracts. It does not include trading profits.

Section 552 defines a foreign personal holding company as a company having 60% of its income being foreign personal holding company income, which includes not only the items in personal holding company income, but capital gains from share dealing and commodity dealing, and from dealing in interests in trusts. A further definition is that "at any time during the taxable year, more than 50% in value of its outstanding stock is owned directly, or indirectly by or for not more than five individuals who are citizens or residents of the U.S." Again, we have this troublesome problem of the definition of the word "stock," and the idea of the valuation of stock.

Finally, we have to consider Sub-Part F, relating to Controlled Foreign Corporations. We have already looked at some of the definitions in Sections 957 and 958.

Section 951 obliges a U.S. shareholder in such a company to report such income attributed to him or her, as is defined as Sub-Part F income. This includes passive income, as already noted, and profits from transactions where one of the parties is related to the corporation. We do not need to expand on this. If a shareholder steers a deal into the company, even though it is constructed to look like an independent transaction, this section simply views it at the true origin of the profits.

This can conclude our examination of this particular problem. If a guarantee company is taxed as a corporation, it would seem, prima facie, that since there is no stock there is no reporting requirement. Yet, there is no certainty. If the IRS determines otherwise, the company will be treated like any share-issuing company. Let us now look at the trust situation.

For tax purposes, a trust's central feature is its objective in protecting and conserving the assets placed in it. The beneficiaries cannot share in this duty, as that is the function of the trustees. The beneficiaries are not, therefore, associates in a joint enterprise for the conduct of a business for profit. Clearly, if we are considering a hybrid company, where the non-shareholder members have no voting power, but where they are entitled to all the income and capital rights, the parallel with a trust is such that there is little doubt that a hybrid company would be considered a constructive trust, and therefore has to be structured with this in mind.

Section 679 of the IRC state, "A United States person who directly or indirectly transfers property to a foreign trust shall be treated as the owner for his taxable year of the portion of such trust attributable to such property if for such year there is a United States beneficiary of any portion of such trust."

The only exceptions to this are where the transfer arises as a result of the death of the transferor, (i.e. it is set up under the will, or where the transfer is for a consideration at arms-length valuation and the whole of the consideration is paid at the time.)

This inevitably leads one to the belief that where a U.S. resident or citizen transfers assets by way of subscription to a company limited by guarantee, or a hybrid company that is deemed by the IRS as a constructive trust, and either that citizens or other U.S. Taxpayers are members of the company, Clause 679 will apply. However, there are ways of coping with this.

For example, if there really were no U.S. beneficiaries, but instead, we were to set up some non-U.S. Person or fund as the beneficiary, such as the Venice in Peril Committee, we could protect the company from Section 679, while still enabling us to pass on benefits to the client.

So, in conclusion, we can recognize that while guarantee and hybrid companies can be a fascinating tool for U.S. tax planning, they have to be handled very carefully, and with precision. By careful structuring we can determine their taxable status and thus we are able to design them very precisely to achieve very precise objectives.

Conclusion

By now, it should be clear that these fascinating forms of corporate vehicle can have a multiplicity of uses. However, a word of caution: these are relatively new concepts in tax planning. There are many uncertainties. It is strongly recommended that great care is taken before using them. It is not enough to ring up your friendly company formation agent and order one off the shelf. For a start, there probably will not be any on the shelf. Secondly, each must be tailor-made to the circumstances of each client. Where should you go? Jurisdictions that have been used are Gibraltar, Cayman Islands, Isle of Man, and British Virgin Islands.

Appendix II
The Cayman Islands

A Base for International Finance and Insurance

Many of the readers of my expanded notes are convinced that the Caribbean Islands offer the best offshore jurisdiction for setting up and operating a foreign-based business. This may have been true in the past, but recently with the threat of drug traffic and money-laundering based in that area, legitimate business operations sometimes are painted with the same illegal and dangerous brush.

For this reason we do not generally suggest to our clients that they select a Caribbean Island country for an offshore jurisdiction. There are instances, however, when the type of business and the economic substructure of the island dictate the need to take a second look. For many reasons the Cayman Islands offer some definite advantages. So for the sake of those who must choose the islands of the Caribbean, here are some of the details on the Cayman Islands.

General Background

The Cayman Islands are a group of three islands, Grand Cayman, Cayman Brac, and Little Cayman, lying south of Cuba and northwest of Jamaica.

Geography and Climate

All three islands are projecting peaks of the Cayman Ridge, a range of submarine mountains in the Caribbean Sea. Although the islands are extremely low-lying and lack the lush vegetation of other tropical islands, they are largely reef protected and offer excellent opportunities for all water sports, especially scuba diving. The beaches are unspoiled and the waters crystal-clear.

George Town is the capital and the center of government and most business activity. George Town is located on Grand Cayman. The island has a resident population of 19,000 and an area of approximately 76 square miles. The other two islands are smaller and have a combined population of about 1, 600. Tourism attractions are limited in keeping with the islands' quiet and peaceful atmosphere.

The climate is tropical with a cooler season between November and April due to the prevailing trade winds.

Government and Constitution

The Cayman Islands are a British Crown Colony. Under the present constitution, introduced in 1972, the islands enjoy a large measure of self-government. This constitution vests executive and legislative power and the responsibility for the administration of the islands in a governor, an executive council and a Legislative Assembly.

The governor is appointed by the British government and acts as president of the Legislative Assembly and chair of the executive council. The assembly consists of three senior civil servants and 12 elected members who serve for a four year term as representatives of the various districts of the islands. No formal political parties have yet developed.

The executive council is made up of three official members, appointed by the governor, and four of the elected members of the Legislative Assembly, chosen by their fellow elected members for a four year term. Individual members have areas of responsibilities as designated by the governor and as a council is responsible for initiating legislation that must be passed by the Legislative Assembly to become law.

Thus, the Cayman Islands are entirely responsible for passing their own laws and intervention by the British government is only possible should the governor seek its approval to act against the advice or wish of executive council. The islands have traditionally enjoyed stable government under the present constitution. There is no desire for independence and no major racial or political problems have arisen.

The Economy

As well as being politically stable, the Cayman Islands enjoy a buoyant economy. The two major fields of business activity are tourism and the offshore financial business conducted in the islands. Both types of business activity generate some direct government revenue. The revenue is generated through a low hotel tax, incorporation and annual fees for all registered companies, with additional license fees for banks, trust companies, and insurance companies. The greatest economic benefits brought to the Cayman Islands by these industries have

267

been full employment and major projects for the local construction industry. The major projects center on tourist development, such as modern office blocks, hotels, and condominiums.

The economic strengths of the islands are reflected in annual budget surpluses, full employment, and a high standard of living. The standard of living is probably one of the highest in the Caribbean.

There is no income or profit taxes on companies or individuals and no inheritance taxes or estate duties. The principal sources of government revenue, in addition to those already indicated, are customs duties (generally 20%) on virtually all imported goods, and stamp duties, particularly on property transactions (7 1/2% of property sale values).

The Legal System

The law of the Cayman Islands is based on English law, together with local statutes that have generally modernized and modified common law in a way suitable for the local business environment.

Currency

The currency of the Cayman Islands is the Cayman Islands dollar, which is fixed to the U.S. dollar at the rate of U.S. $1.20 = C.I. $1.00. There are no restrictions on the use of U.S. currency within the Cayman Islands.

Cayman Islands as an Offshore Business and Finance Center

Since the mid-1960s, the Cayman Islands have developed rapidly as a base for offshore finance and business operations and they now enjoy international recognition as a stable and reputable center. There are more than 25,000 companies, 540 licensed banks and trust companies, including branches and subsidiaries of most of the world's largest banking institutions, and 350 licensed insurance companies. The principal reasons for this development include:

- Absence of all forms of direct taxation.

- Continued political and economic stability as a British Crown Colony.

- A convenient companies law with minimum restrictions, and facilities for speedy company incorporation and registration.

- Confidentiality of all business activities and information. Disclosure of confidential client information without prior client permission to persons or agencies within or outside the Cayman Islands is a criminal offense under the Confidential Relationship (Preservation) Law, 1979.

The one exception to this is contained in the Narcotic Drug (Evidence) (United States of America) Law, 1984. Under this legislation, if the attorney general of the United States requires information about proceedings or investigations into narcotic activities, he or she may request the attorney general of the Cayman Islands to procure relevant documents or information. Any person divulging such information or documents will not be

269

deemed to have committed any offense under the Confidential Relationship (Preservation) Law, the Banks and Trust Companies Regulation Law (Revised) or any other law in force in the Cayman Islands. There are safeguards in the law to ensure that information so obtained may not be used for any purpose other than the narcotics-related grounds set out in the original request from the U.S. attorney general.

This is seen to be a positive measure by the government to demonstrate its opposition to drug-related activities, and it is not expected to affect adversely the traditional financial and business operations of the islands. The extent of the exchange of information with the United States is to be extended by the Mutual Legal Assistance Treaty, which, although approved by the Cayman Islands government has yet to be ratified by the U.S. senate.

- Extensive professional infrastructure; including international banks and trust companies, insurance management companies, law firms with international reputations, and international accounting firms.

- Good communications; direct air service with Miami and Houston, United States, and Kingston, Jamaica, excellent international telephone, fax and telex lines, and reliable postal and courier services.

- Absence of any foreign exchange controls or restrictions.

- Friendliness of the local population to the tourist and business person alike.

General Incorporation and Company Requirements

The dynamic expansion of the Cayman Islands as an offshore tax haven is exemplified by the increase in the number of companies registered in the islands, from under 300 at the end of 1968 to over 25,000 on March 31, 1992. Companies incorporated in the Cayman Islands are regulated by the Cayman Islands Companies Law. The principal documents of incorporation are the Memorandum and Articles of Association, which should contain the following information:

Memorandum of Association

Under the Companies Law, the following specific matters must be dealt with in the Memorandum of Association.

1. Name of the company.

2. The registered office.

3. Statement of the limitation of liability of the members, unless it is an unlimited company.

4. The share capital of the company, if it is limited by shares.

5. The minimum government incorporation fee allows for a share capital of up to $960,000, U.S. dollars ($900,000, U.S. dollars for an exempted company), which is, therefore, the authorized share capital most commonly chosen by companies. There are no minimum capitalization requirements (other than for banks, trust companies and insurance companies).

Articles of Association

The Articles of Association regulate the internal management of the affairs of the company and are equivalent to bylaws in the United States. Unless specifically excluded, the Articles of Association set out in Table A to the Companies Law will be deemed to govern a company. The articles govern such matters as the powers and duties of directors, the issue of shares, and the procedures for meetings.

Company incorporation is controlled by the Registrar of Companies with whom the Memorandum and Articles of Association must be filed, together with a register of directors and officers. Incorporation can usually be completed in under a week. If urgent, it may be accomplished in a shorter period.

There is a minimum amount of information required to incorporate a Cayman Islands company.

Ordinary Companies

An ordinary company is any company that is not an exempted company. It is subject to the following requirements.

- A minimum of one shareholder.

- A minimum of one director and a company secretary.

- The name must be displayed outside the registered office.

- The annual general meeting must be held at least once every calendar year, with not more than 15 months between meetings.

- In January of each year, an annual return giving details of capital structure and shareholders must be filed with the Registrar of Companies.

- Ordinary companies may be designated non-resident, in which case a certificate is required to this effect from the Registrar of Companies. The company must carry on its business primarily outside the islands. Such companies are not required to have a director resident in the Cayman Islands.

Exempted Companies

An exempted company, the vehicle most often used for offshore business, is incorporated in the same way as an ordinary company but is subject to different requirements and enjoys the following exemptions.

- It does not have to file the Annual Return and list required for ordinary companies.

- It does not have to hold an annual general meeting of members.

- It may issue negotiable or bearer shares.

- It may obtain an exemption from future Cayman taxes (usually granted for a period of 20 years.)

- The name of the company may be in a foreign language and need not include the world "Limited" or the abbreviation "Ltd."

However, an exempted company is subject to the following requirements.

- It must file an Annual Return and Declaration in January of each year.

273

- At least one director is required, but directors need not be residents of the Cayman Islands.

- At least one directors' meeting must be held in the Cayman Islands each year, either in person or by proxy, subject to the Articles of Association.

- It may not engage in local business in the Cayman Islands.

- It may not make any invitation to the public in the islands to subscribe for its shares.

An exempted company enjoys more confidentiality than an ordinary company because it is required to disclose less information to the Registrar of Companies.

Foreign Companies

A company incorporated in another jurisdiction that establishes a place of business or carries on business from within the islands must register with the Registrar of Companies. To do so, it must provide the following documentation.

- Certified copy of its Memorandum and Articles of Association and Certificate of Incorporation, or equivalent foreign documents.

- Certified copy of the list of directors.

- The names and addresses of persons resident in the islands who are authorized to accept service of process on behalf of the company.

Government Fees

As with all offshore jurisdictions, Cayman Islands companies are required to pay an initial incorporation fee and annual fee to the government. These differ for ordinary and exempted companies. The fees involved will be quoted at the time of inquiry to assure accuracy.

It should be noted that such fees are subject to change by the government from time to time, and current fee scales are always available on request.

Statutory Requirements

Registers and Books of Account

The Companies Law requires that the following statutory records be maintained at the registered office of the company.

Register of Members

> This register must include the names and addresses of all members, together with the number of shares held and the date on which the person became or ceased to be a member.

Register of Mortgages and Charges

> This register must record all mortgages and charges affecting property of the company. The register includes details of the property mortgaged or charged, the amount of charge created and the names of the mortgagees or persons entitled to the charge. This register shall be open for inspection by any member or creditor of the company.

Register of Directors

This register must include the names and addresses of all directors and officers of the company. Any changes must be notified to the Registrar within 30 days.

Books of Account

Every company must keep Books of Account sufficient to give a true and fair view of the state of the company's affairs and to explain its transactions. Specifically, the following items must be included in the Books of Account.

- All money received and spent by the company, including the sources of receipts and nature of expenditures.

- All sales and purchase of goods by the company

- The assets and liabilities of the company.

With the exception of licensed banks, trust companies, insurance companies and company management companies, the Cayman Islands' law does not require annual financial statements to be produced, or, if produced, to be audited. However, the following formalities have to be observed:

- An annual return and list or declaration must be submitted to the Registrar of Companies in January of each year.

- The annual fee must accompany the annual return.

- The Registrar of Companies must be informed, within the prescribed time limit, when the company changes it's Articles or Memorandum of Association to effect any of the following.

    1. A change of name.

    2. A change of registered office.

    3. A change of directors or officers.

    4. An increase in its authorized share capital.

Where such changes require a special resolution, copies of such must be filed with the Registrar of Companies within the prescribed time limit.

Striking-Off

If a company does not pay its annual fee, or if the Registrar of Companies has reason to believe a company is not carrying on business, the Registrar may strike it from the register. This is also an inexpensive and convenient way to dissolve an inactive company because the directors may request the Registrar to take such action. To do so, the directors of the company must certify that the company is inactive and that it has no assets or liabilities.

It should be noted that if the company has any assets at the time of striking-off, those assets vest in the treasury of the Cayman Islands and any aggrieved creditor or member may apply to court to have the company reinstated. In addition, under the provisions of the law the striking-off of a company from the register does not affect the liability, if any, of any director, officer or member of the company, which can only be achieved by the due process of liquidation.

Typical Uses of Cayman Islands Companies

Many Cayman Islands companies are established to legally meet the objective of minimizing, deferring, or avoiding taxation in other jurisdictions. Comprehensive advice on such matters is not, however, generally available in the Cayman Islands. Competent international tax planning advice should always be sought in the jurisdictions in which the owner, whether a company or an individual, is doing business and is resident for tax purposes.

Some of the more common uses of Cayman Islands companies include the following.

- Offshore banking and trust companies.

- Offshore insurance and reinsurance companies. This is one of the best jurisdictions for offshore captive insurance companies.

- Offshore investment companies, investment holding companies and mutual funds.

- International trading, leasing or servicing companies.

- Companies generating international royalties and commissions.

Corporate Management

A considerable number of companies do not maintain a physical presence in the islands. Many banks, trust companies, attorneys, accountants, and corporate management companies provide facilities for registered offices. They will also maintain the required statutory records for registered offices.

In addition, the services of directors or nominee share-holders may also be provided to hold the necessary meetings required by law.

Even though it may be desirable for international tax planning reasons, it is not common practice these days for such management entities to provide directors unless they are in a position to execute properly their legal responsibilities to manage and control a company's affairs. To do so, a director must ensure that all transactions effected by the company are bona fide and in its best interests.

Many accounting firms in the Cayman Islands offer corporate management services, primarily for their existing clients. Intercon Associates, Ltd. of the Isle of Man will assist interested clients in securing the services of a competent chartered accountant.

Local Companies (Control) Law

Any company that wishes to engage in local business, whether an ordinary company or a foreign company registered in the islands, must be licensed to do so by the Communion Protection Board under the Cayman Islands Local Companies (Control) Law, and the Trades and Business Licensing Law.

The licenses are granted at the discretion of the Caymanian Protection Board, but usually require substantial Caymanian participation. If the Caymanian participation is 60% or more, the company is classified as a Cayman company and obtains a license as a matter of course.

Management Companies

Under the Companies Management Law (1984), no company (unless licensed under the Banks and Trust Companies Regulation Law) may carry on the business of company management without a license. Such business is defined as the provision of managerial services for profit or reward, the provision of directors, or when the control of the whole or substantial assets of the company is vested in the management company. There are exceptions where services are limited to the provision of a registered office and nominee shareholders.

The basic provisions of the law are the following.

- An Inspector of Company Managers to supervise management companies.

- Licensees must have insurance against claims arising from negligence or breach of duty.

- Annual financial statements of the company managers must be audited.

- Paid-up share capital must be more than CI $25,000.

Where the governor is of the opinion that a licensee is carrying on business in contravention of the law, or in a manner detrimental to the public interest, the governor may suspend or revoke the license. Appeal against suspension or revocation lies with the Grand Court.

Winding-Up

The winding-up or liquidation of the company is also controlled by the Companies Law. Liquidation may be of two types: voluntary, by resolution of the shareholders, or compulsory, by order of the court.

Compulsory liquidation is usually granted by the court on an application by a petitioning creditor. In both cases a liquidator is appointed. The liquidator assumes control of all the assets of the company and is responsible for receiving claims from creditors of the company and distributing the assets to creditors and shareholders in accordance with the Companies Law.

Banks and Trust Companies

The costs associated with capitalization and fees associated with establishing a bank in the Cayman Islands have served to reduce the number of new banks over the last few years. There are less expensive jurisdictions, though there are few better equipped to handle the offshore banking business you may require.

As of December 31, 1987, there were 508 banks and trust companies licensed in the Cayman Islands. Of these, 32 held Category "A" licenses (permitting domestic and offshore operations) and 476 held Class B licenses (permitting offshore operations only). Forty-two of the world's 50 largest banks are represented in the Cayman Islands.

Continuing links with the United Kingdom (as a British Crown Colony), political stability, and the absence of taxation and exchange controls are considered to be the main factors contributing to the continued growth of the banking and related financial industry. The Cayman Islands Government remains vigilant in processing applications for bank and trust company licenses, and through its requirements for the annual submission of audited financial statements, seeks to prevent disreputable or unsound banking practices.

Advantages of the Cayman Islands for Banks and Trusts

Apart from the general advantages of doing business in the Cayman Islands, some specific benefits applicable to banking and trust operations include the following.

- Relative freedom from controls on international banking and trust activities.

- Access to international Eurocurrency markets and the unfettered ability to carry out Eurodollar transactions.

- Absence of exchange controls.

- Absence of stringent regulations on liquidity ratios and capital requirements.

- Profits may be retained offshore, and repatriated at will, with the possible advantage of legally reducing or postponing payment of taxes in the home country of the parent.

- Interest can be paid without deduction of tax at source.

- The ability to provide trust facilities for clients and customers.

Types of Business Engaged In
By Cayman-Based Banks and Trusts

Types of business currently carried on include:

- Eurocurrency borrowing and lending.

- Deposit taking and placing.

- Bond and floating rate note issues.

- Consortium lending and group financing.

- Discounting promissory notes.

- Branch banking.

- Provision of financial services for private clients.

- Trust business.

- International fiduciary and corporate services.

Licensing Requirements

In order to do business in the Cayman Islands, banks and trust companies must be licensed under the Banks and Trust Companies Regulation Law, 1966. Without a license, no company may transact any banking or trust business or use any word in its name like bank, trust, savings and loan, etc.

The procedures for obtaining a banking or trust license is fairly complex. Intercon Associates, Ltd. will complete the procedure subject to a full review of the desire of the client and consultation with our affiliated companies in the Cayman Islands.

Real Estate and Office Location

The past decade has seen an unprecedented increase in both construction activity and the prices paid for land and buildings. Beach front property on Seven Mile Beach, the islands' premier beach location, can cost up to $12,000 U.S. dollars per front foot for a prime site. A typical two-bedroom condominium on the beach would start at about $150,000 U.S. dollars, and luxury developments are now reaching over $1,000,000 U.S. dollars per unit.

Systems of land registration

All land that has a registered title is designated a registration number and block and parcel number. These are recorded in the Register of Titles, which also includes details of any charges or other encumbrances over the land. The advantage of this system is that title to property may be readily ascertained without the need to trace a title to its origins.

Strata Corporation

The Strata Titles Law, passed in 1973, made it possible for a registered title to be obtained to a self-contained unit that formed part of a larger building. Upon registration of a Strata Plan, the proprietors automatically become a body corporate and have the statutory duty, inter alia, to ensure that the buildings are insured and properly maintained.

Establishing an Office in the Cayman Islands

If a company wishes to establish a permanent place of business in the islands, there are several factors to be considered. The principal consideration is the location of the office space and recruitment of suitable staff.

The recent construction of office complexes has made office space readily available in George Town. Air-conditioned offices in modern premises rent for approximately $30-35 U.S. dollars per square foot per year. Leases are usually for a minimum of one year.

There are two categories of staff, local and expatriate. There are no restrictions on employment of local staff, although the Cayman Islands enjoy full employment and there is a shortage of trained local staff, particularly secretarial and professional.

Expatriate staff (non-Caymanians) require Gainful Occupation Licenses (work permits), which are issued subject to the non-availability of suitable local staff to fill a particular position. The government is anxious, however, to ensure that wherever possible local staff is trained to fill employment positions at all levels of responsibility.

Gainful Occupation Licenses must be obtained for expatriates before arrival in the islands. The annual cost of these is $600 U.S. dollars for secretarial staff, $900 U.S. dollars for administrative staff, $1,800 U.S. dollars for assistant managers, and $2,400 U.S. dollars for managers, partners, and company directors.

Rental accommodation is available for expatriate staff, in either houses or condominiums. Rents tend to be high and can vary from $1,000 to $2,500 U.S. dollars a month, depending upon size, location, and degree of luxury provided. A modern two-bedroom condominium on the beach would be between $1,400 to $1,800 U.S. dollars a month. Most accommodations are fully furnished.

A car is considered essential in the Cayman Islands, as public transportation is limited. Careful consideration should be given to employee costs, as this item will figure significantly in budgeting the cost of local operations. Staff salaries are somewhat higher than in the United States or Europe, reflecting the high cost of living. However, all remuneration is untaxed in the islands. In addition, senior staff is often provided with free accommodations and a car, together with annual return airfares home and medical insurance.

The Cayman Islands Captive Insurance Industry

The Cayman Islands are now widely recognized as the one of the most popular domiciles for offshore captive insurance companies after Bermuda, the traditional center of the offshore insurance industry. By the end of 1986, 444 offshore insurance companies had been licensed under the Cayman Islands' Insurance Law, 1979, and total applications numbered 590.

An analysis of the types of licensed insurers indicates the following:

44% traditional captives; 31% association or industry captives; approximately 20% of the companies are privately owned insurance and reinsurance companies with a limited book of business and only limited commercial activity; 4% are open market reinsurers of varying sizes; and 1% are life companies.

Classes of business covered by those licensed, generally taking the form of reinsurance rather than direct writing, are widely spread. The principal ones are as follows.

Casualty: Including workers' compensation, comprehensive general liability, medical malpractice, products liability, automobile damage and warranty.

Property: Including material damage and business interruption.

Life: Including life assurance of all kinds, credit life, and credit health and accident.

The Cayman Islands have experienced significant growth in offshore insurance business since the mid-1970s. The introduction of the Cayman Islands' Insurance Law, 1979 has contributed to this but the principal reasons include those listed previously in relation to the growth of the Cayman Islands as an offshore financial center.

The existing reputation as a stable domicile and center for international banking, and the presence of a sound professional infrastructure that had already developed to serve these industries, is the primary reason for the development of the Cayman Islands as an insurance center.

In addition to the licensed offshore insurers, 28 underwriting managers had been licensed by the end of 1986. Fourteen (14) of the managers had established a local presence, and several reinsurance brokerage operations are now established.

It is expected that the growth in licensed insurers will be sustained. This, together with the existence of the reinsurance brokers and several "open market" reinsurers, will enhance the Cayman Islands' reputation as an offshore insurance center. Resulting in an increasing exchange of business between the Cayman Islands and other more mature insurance centers.

Because the captive insurance industry is so well established in the Cayman Islands, we wish to use this section to outline in more detail the structure and use of captive insurance companies.

The Cayman Islands and Bermuda stand out as one of the best jurisdictions for captive insurance. The Isle of Man is also an outstanding jurisdiction, as well as the Channel Islands and several other business havens around the world.

Background Information and Definitions

The captive insurance industry is now recognized by the international financial and business world as a significant and integral part of the international insurance market. It has developed, essentially over the last 20 to 30 years, as an alternative provider of protection, particularly for the multinational corporation, against the risk of damage or loss and third-party liabilities.

The feature that distinguishes the captive insurance company from the traditional insurance company is the restricted nature of the risks that it underwrites or reinsures, whether these are the risks of its parent company, shareholders, or a particular selection of international reinsurance business.

Many of the early captives were incorporated in the 1920's and 1930's on a co-insurance or mutual basis in the United Kingdom and North America. Recently, several states in the United States have introduced favorable legislation to promote the growth of domestic captives.

However, a significant number of such companies are now incorporated in offshore financial centers, which offer a number of advantages, including the following.

- Less restrictive insurance regulation.

- Freedom from exchange control.

- Absent or low rates of taxation. Both domestic and offshore captives fall into a number of categories, including:

Parent-Only or Pure Captive

A wholly owned or controlled company that only insures or reinsures the risks of its non-insurance parent or affiliated companies.

Association or Industry Captive

An insurance company owned by a group of industrial or commercial companies or members of a professional association solely to insure or reinsure the risks of their shareholders. (This category includes industry pools where the risks of all shareholders are pooled and ceded back to participants of the pool on a shared basis.)

Agency Captive

An insurance company owned by insurance brokers or agents who reinsure a portion of the insurance they sell with their own captive insurance company.

Quasi Profit Center or Open Market Captive

A subsidiary that primarily insures or reinsures the risk of its parent or affiliated companies but, at the same time, insures the risks of unrelated parties or assumes open market reinsurance business (usually by quota share participation in a reinsurance pool).

Captives may be established as direct-writing companies issuing policies to, and receiving premiums from, their insured—in other words, operating on much the same basis as the conventional insurance company.

However, in many jurisdictions, the insurance industry is highly regulated and legislation often requires that certain lines of insurance can only be underwritten by companies that have satisfied local regulations (known as admitted or registered carriers). Such regulations would probably include capital and surplus requirements and involve onerous filings and registrations and detailed annual reporting requirements.

For these reasons, most offshore captives are established as reinsurance companies whereby a domestic insurer (i.e., an admitted or registered carrier) writes the primary policy for the risks of the captive's parent and then cedes all or part of the risk to the captive. Under such an arrangement, the admitted or registered carrier is commonly referred to as the "fronting" company.

The captive may retain all the risk and premium that it assumes, or it may retrocede a proportion of the reinsurance assumed to another reinsurance company. In practice, it is not uncommon for an offshore captive to operate as a direct-writer and also as a reinsurer for those lines of business that it is precluded from writing directly.

Because of the explosion in litigation on insurance claims and the large settlements or awards that accompanies these in the United States, there has been a tremendous growth of the captive insurance industry.

Recent surveys indicate that there are probably in excess of 1,500 active captives throughout the world (although precise estimates are difficult because, in many offshore domiciles, such information is not a matter of public record and may be subject to protection under confidentiality laws).

At least 30% of the Fortune 500 companies have a captive insurance subsidiary. Captives located in the United States, Bermuda, the Cayman Islands, and the Channel Islands wrote almost $7.5 billion U.S. dollars in premiums in 1985.

The principal reasons for this growth have been not only the positive benefits and advantages to be derived from offshore captives (as discussed in the following section), but the various problems and difficulties experienced by the insurance industry itself.

The reasons for forming captive insurance companies are varied and, while it is commonly thought that tax minimization or deferral is the primary reason, this is frequently not the case in practice. The principal reasons for captive formation are listed below. It will usually be necessary for more than one of these reasons to exist before formation of a captive may be considered advantageous.

1. Cost Reductions: Probably the most common reason for establishing a captive is to minimize costs of risk management. Insurance purchased in the conventional market obviously includes a portion of the insurer's overhead and profits, which may be as high as 40% of the premium. Although not all of these costs are avoided by the establishment of a captive, they should be reduced and, if the captive's own loss experience is no worse and claims handling costs are no greater than the average of the conventional insurer's business, then the captive should be left with an underwriting profit.

    In addition, the offshore captive may substantially reduce, or even avoid, other expenses such as administration and settlement of claims, loss control expenses,

291

various states and federal taxes, brokerage commissions and other acquisition costs, and consulting fees.

The actual premium cost of certain high risk or "long-tail" insurance (such as products liability or medical malpractice) has been successfully contained by association or industry captives, formed for the purpose of avoiding the volatility of market cycles.

2. Insuring the Uninsurable: The insurance industry is subject to considerable cyclical changes in which excess capacity leads to competition, resulting in decreased premium rates and poor underwriting capacity, which may cause some types of cover to be unavailable until increased premiums re-establish a market.

   This sudden unavailability of the required cover may cause insured persons to contemplate the establishment of a captive, but some captives have been formed because the coverage required, for example for a new or potentially hazardous product, is either unavailable in the conventional market or is only available at an unacceptably high price. Other such examples include cover for environmental pollution, medical malpractice, and natural catastrophes.

3. Stability of Market: As described above, the traditional insurance market is subjected to cyclical changes. These changes occur when the required cover may be unobtainable or unacceptably expensive. A captive creates a stable base where the insured can be confident of obtaining cover at a reasonable price irrespective of the commercial market forces.

4. Risk Retention, Risk Management and Loss Control: The assumption or retention of its own risk within certain limits is attractive to a company with a better loss history than its industry average. For the types of risk

where self-insurance is not permitted and tax deductibility is not available, an offshore captive reinsurer may enable a company to achieve these objectives, subject to reasonable fronting costs.

The opportunity to centralize and tailor a company's risk management programs and improve loss control efficiency is an important, but often overlooked, reason for establishing a captive. This is particularly applicable to diversified corporate groups and companies with significant products liability or safety risks.

5. Cash Flow Benefits: The insurance industry has traditionally relied upon high investment income to supplement modest or even negative underwriting results. Such investment income is generated primarily from funds represented by unearned premiums and unpaid losses, as premiums are usually paid in advance, often annually, while claims tend to be paid out over a period, the length of which depends on the type of business.

Assuming that a captive is adequately capitalized for the business which it is writing, the timing of premium receipts and reinsurance payments can be planned, and loss reserving policies determined, to maximize investment income. On a consolidated basis, the parent company, rather than the conventional insurer, accumulates the benefit. Moreover, for offshore captives in tax-free domiciles, there is the possible added advantage of generating investment income on untaxed funds.

6. Access to the Reinsurance Market: A fundamental benefit resulting from establishing a captive is its ability to gain access into the international reinsurance market, the wholesale market for insurance. Thus captives can often obtain reinsurance, which is less expensive than

conventional direct excess and umbrella cover.

In addition, the captive has the opportunity to reduce costs by combining two or more lines of risk and may earn ceding and/or profit commission. However, international reinsurance companies look for long-term relationships and therefore carefully evaluate a captive's underwriting performance and the management and financial position of its parent prior to entering any agreement.

7. Diversification into Profit Center: Another reason for establishing a captive is to diversify into open market insurance services and operate as a separate commercial profit center. Whereas the primary reason for forming a parent-only captive is usually to reduce insurance costs, an ancillary benefit may be the generation of profits from outside or unrelated business.

   However, the underwriting of such business could also expose the company to underwriting losses. Successful examples of such captives indicate that some underwriting control by the parent, including professional selection of business underwritten, is desirable.

8. "Unbundling" of Services: Usually an ancillary, rather than primary, reason for forming a captive is that a company may not be satisfied with the technical services provided by its conventional insurer and may wish to "unbundle" risk control and claims handling services from the actual purchase of insurance cover.

9. Reduction of Government Regulations and Restrictions: As already indicated, the insurance industry is heavily regulated in all developed economies. These include minimum capital and surplus requirements, solvency margins, specific ratios of premiums written to net assets (and, in particular, loss reserving requirements)

and, in some cases, restrictions on investments.

In addition, many multinational corporations experience difficulties in international transfer of funds through dividend payments because of national exchange control restrictions. An offshore location for a captive insurance or reinsurance company can, if properly established within the legal requirements of the place of domicile, provide a less onerous regulatory environment, widen investment opportunities, and facilitate legitimate international movements of funds that may be of vital importance to the commercial interests of the multinational corporation.

10. Tax Minimization and Deferral: As indicated above, the establishment of a captive insurance company should always be determined by its viability as an insurance operation, independent of any tax advantage, which should be viewed as an incidental, but nevertheless significant, benefit. There are, however, a number of possible tax advantages. These tax advantages may be briefly summarized as follows.

A. The accumulation of tax-free underwriting and investment earnings by use of qualifying offshore captives, subject to the holding of such earnings outside the parent company's country of residence for tax purposes.

B. The use of an offshore or foreign captive may allow a company to utilize foreign tax credits which would otherwise expire (this does not apply, however, to tax-free offshore domiciles).

Tax considerations apply to the parent (i.e., essentially whether or not its premiums paid to the captive are deductible for domestic purposes) and to the captive itself. These depend very much on its location and its

295

ability to defer the repatriation of earnings back to its parent, which will normally result in deferral of any tax liability.

The subject of using captives in international tax planning strategy is a complex one and anti-avoidance tax legislation exists in most developed countries (including the United States, the United Kingdom, Japan, and Germany). Consequently, expert legal and tax advice should always be sought in advance of incorporating a captive, in a particular jurisdiction and in the country where the parent is domiciled for tax purposes.

Other Alternatives

The use of a captive may not always be the most appropriate method of risk management. Other alternatives may deserve serious consideration depending upon particular circumstances, including the following.

- A self-insurance program which may result in cost reductions and improved cash flow. Although, as already indicated, for some lines of business this alternative may not be allowed by domestic legislation and may not be tax effective even if treated as a deductible expense for tax purposes.

- The use of a retrospective rating plan policy where an initial or deposit premium is paid and then retrospectively adjusted based on actual loss experience of the insured. The purpose of this type of policy is to delay premium payments and thereby achieve cash flow benefits; such rating plans can be very complex but may be a suitable alternative for general liability insurance.

- Optimum use of deductions, which may be available from direct insurers in exchange for a discount from the basic premium rate.

Feasibility Studies

A detailed feasibility study should always be prepared and preferably should include proper consideration of all of the available alternatives. A feasibility study that concludes that the establishment of a captive is the best alternative would normally require that most, if not all, of the following criteria have been satisfied.

- A level of capitalization and premium volume that will make the captive financially viable, taking into account the class of business involved, anticipated loss exposure, set up expenses, and operating costs.

- Efficient risk management and loss control. It is particularly important that this evaluation has been made accurately and objectively by qualified professionals.

- Reliable fronting arrangements and good quality reinsurance, which may not necessarily be those offered at the lowest cost.

- Commitment from the parent's management to support the captive with adequate finance and expertise.

- The availability of competent management services to operate the captive, whether such services are provided by independent managers or from within the parent itself.

Criteria for Location of a Captive

The principal considerations will depend upon the relative importance attached to the general business and economic aspects, tax considerations, and the geographical convenience of location.

As already indicated, the fundamental decision is whether to form a domestic captive (where allowed by local regulations) or an offshore captive. In considering the use of an offshore domicile the following features will be important.

- Political and economic stability.

- The existence of a flexible and acceptable legal and regulatory framework.

- Tax-free status or reciprocal tax treaties, depending upon particular tax planning objectives.

- Availability of competent local management and professional and business services.

- Absence of exchange controls and ability to transact business in principal international trading currencies.

- Convenient air services and good communications.

Reasons for Development

The Cayman Islands have experienced significant growth in offshore insurance business since the mid-1970s. The introduction of the Cayman Islands' Insurance Law, 1979 has contributed to this, but the principal reasons include those listed previously in relation to the growth of the Cayman Islands as an offshore financial center.

As an illustration of the use of a jurisdiction for captive insurance, we will detail the Cayman Islands as a typical offshore jurisdiction that has concentrated its efforts on the insurance industry.

Bermuda is still the primary insurance haven of the world. The Isle of Man and the Channel Islands have a strong following among European business advisors. Each jurisdiction has its advantages but all are similar to a certain degree.

The Cayman Islands' Insurance Law, 1979

Objectives and Philosophy

The Cayman Islands government had two basic objectives in introducing this law: First, to codify regulations to cover the operations of domestic insurers with the primary objective of protecting the interests of local policyholders; and second, it was designed to encourage the development of offshore insurance business while, at the same time, ensuring that the islands' reputation as an offshore financial center would not be brought into disrepute.

The law, therefore, introduced licensing requirements for all insurers, brokers, agents, and underwriting managers. For insurers there are two principal license categories: the Class "A" license for companies carrying on domestic insurance in the Cayman Islands; and Class "B", either restricted or unrestricted, for offshore companies.

The concept of the restricted license was intended for companies underwriting parent business only and such licensees must give an undertaking to insure or reinsure risks of shareholders only. However, almost 80% of Class "B" licenses issued are unrestricted.

The law also established the position of the Superintendent of Insurance, who is charged with the responsibility of reviewing and processing all applications and supervising compliance with annual reporting requirements. Supporting regulations (The Insurance (Forms) Regulations, 1980) set out the prescribed format of all license applications, the Certificate of Compliance, and the auditors' confirmation that audited financial statements have been prepared.

License Application Information

The following is a brief summary of information required for an application for the Class B license.

- The proposed name of the company, which should include a word associated with the insurance business (i.e., insurance, assurance, reinsurance, indemnity, or underwriting).

- The proposed local office in the Cayman Islands where full business records will be kept (subject to the approval of the Superintendent of Insurance, such records may be kept outside the Cayman Islands.)

- Copies of incorporation documents, being the Memorandum and Articles of Association.

- Full details of shareholders, directors and managers, including three references for directors, to include one from a bank and one from the insurance industry

- Written evidence that local auditors and underwriting managers have accepted their appointments (if there is evidence of acceptable underwriting expertise elsewhere, local managers need not be appointed.)

- A business plan detailing the proposed business of the company and indicating the classes of business to be transacted; estimated premium volumes; details of reinsurance outwards; maximum liability to be retained; and, wherever possible, financial projections for at least three years.

- Written evidence of how the net worth requirements will be met. Net worth is defined as excess of assets over liabilities other than liabilities to partners or shareholders. Minimum net worth requirements are as follows.

    1. Companies writing general (property or casualty) business only: $120,000 U.S. dollars.

    2. Companies writing long-term business: $240,000 U.S. dollars.

    3. Companies writing a combination of both general and long-term business: $360,000 U.S. dollars.

It is important to note that it is always preferable that the net worth requirements are satisfied in terms of cash or completely guaranteed notes. Unrestricted Class B insurers should maintain the net worth requirements at all times. Although the regulations exempt the restricted "B" license holder from these requirements, it is unlikely that an application would be approved where proposed net worth was less than $120,000 U.S. dollars.

These net worth requirements are essentially the only ones specified in the law; there are no prescribed premium-to-net asset ratios, solvency requirements or restrictions on investments at the present time, although general industry standards will be considered by the Superintendent in reviewing the application. The Superintendent has the discretionary power to prescribe higher net worth requirements and to set premium-to-net asset ratios.

- Accounting and auditing requirements specify that all licensed insurers must prepare financial statements in accordance with generally accepted accounting principles, which include, inter alia, those principles of the United States, Canada, or the United Kingdom.

Auditors must be appointed. The regulations require that the auditors submit a certificate to the Superintendent within six months of the end of the financial year. This certificate confirms that the annual audited financial statements have been reported on and indicate whether or not the auditors' report was qualified. Audited financial statements already signed by directors are filed with the Superintendent.

In addition, either the insurer's underwriting managers or auditors must complete a Certificate of Compliance within the same time period to confirm that the company has conducted its business in accordance with the business plan, subject to any approved changes, and also that any changes in shareholders, directors and officers have been approved.

Enforcement procedures and penalties are severe; for instance, a licensee may have their license suspended or revoked should the authorities be of the opinion that the licensee is one of the following.

1. Carrying on business in a manner likely to be detrimental to the public interest or to the interest of its creditors or policy holders.

or

2. In contravention of the law, which results in fines of up to $6,000 U.S. dollars or one year's impris-

onment or both. The penalty for making a false representation under the law is a fine of up to $12,000 U.S. dollars or two years' imprisonment or both.

Possible revisions to the law are very likely. The government is presently considering revisions; although these are not expected to result in any significant changes to those sections of the law dealing with the licensing and other requirements for Class-B insurers, the following revisions are under consideration:

1. Reclassification of credit life business when written for periods of less than five years from long-term to general business.

2. Requirement for Class B insurers writing long–term and malpractice business to have annual actuarial valuations.

3. Mandatory filing of annual report by Class B insurers.

4. Powers for the superintendent of insurance to take emergency action in the case of suspected insolvency, (e.g., temporary control of assets and investments).

Association or industry captives

These captives are very common in the Cayman Islands and, because of the diversity of interests in multiple ownership and the need for flexibility in membership, additional considerations must be addressed before organization and incorporation, in particular:

Capital Structure

Under the law, a company may not reduce its issued capital (ordinary shares or common stock) without special approval of the Grand Court, unless the company is put into voluntary liquidation. A Cayman company cannot therefore hold its own shares by, for example, the issue of treasury stock.

Since the process of applying to the Grand Court to reduce share capital is a costly and time-consuming exercise, and since association or industry captives will almost certainly require the flexibility to allow existing members to leave their program, consideration should be given to the provision for the company to issue a special class of shares (redeemable preference shares). Otherwise, the only way one member can leave a program is to transfer his or her shares to a new member, and this may not always be possible.

Should a company wish to issue redeemable preference shares, the ability to do so, the method of issuing and redeeming such shares, and their standing in relationship to other classes of shares should be set out in particular detail in the company's Articles of Association (local legal advice should be sought).

In addition, it is usually advisable to issue such shares at a low nominal or par value with a high premium, since the law also requires that a sum equal to the nominal or par value of shares redeemed must be transferred, out of profits, to a capital redemption reserve fund, which is a non-distributable reserve.

Allocation of net underwriting income to individual shareholders

A feature of association or industry captives that may be attractive to potential participants is that the company's profits can be allocated to shareholders based on the results of their individual underwriting experience.

If this is desired, special provisions should be included in the company's articles of association, clearly setting out the methods of allocation. Local legal advice should be sought to ensure compliance with the law and tax advice should be obtained to ensure that there is bona fide risk sharing. In addition, careful consideration should be given to the special accounting procedures to ensure that there is a proper accounting for, and recording of, such allocations.

Investments

Although the Cayman Islands' Insurance Law, 1979 provides that the Cayman Islands authorities may prescribe that investments of a specified class require the prior approval of the Superintendent of Insurance (this does not apply to restricted Class B license holders), it is assumed that the power to limit investments will only be exercised where this is warranted by the particular circumstances.

The captive's financial statements should disclose the nature of all investments, classify the investments as short-term or long-term, and disclose the basis of their balance sheet value, which will depend to a certain extent on which generally accepted accounting principles are used in the preparation of the financial statements.

A detailed schedule of marketable securities and bonds is usually presented as an accompanying schedule to the financial statements indicating cost, interest rates, maturity dates, and market values where they constitute a significant proportion of the captive's investments.

Consequently, the investment policy of a Cayman Islands captive needs to be carefully considered; in particular to ensure that the liquidity of the investment portfolio is matched with the captive's anticipated future claims payment patterns.

Costs

The cost of incorporating and licensing an insurance company in the Cayman Islands is likely to be in the region of $12,500 to $15,000 U.S. dollars, but could be more, depending on the complexities of its business or capital structure. Annual license and government fees amount to just over $6,000 U.S. dollars.

Accounting and Audit Considerations

Insurance company accounting

In countries where the insurance industry is regulated by specific laws, licensed insurance companies are usually required to prepare, and file with the supervisory agencies of government, annual financial statements prepared in accordance with statutory accounting practices.

Although these practices may vary somewhat from country to country, the method of preparation is basically designed to reflect a company's position from the standpoint of solvency and compliance with minimum capital requirements. Consequently, the balance sheet reflects to a significant extent the net assets of the company, which could be realized on liquidation and which are available to meet outstanding claims.

In addition, it is usual for different accounting practices to apply to different classes of insurance business, principally general business (property and casualty) and long-term business (life assurance). For example, it is normally required that both premium recognition and evaluation of loss reserves for long-term business are based upon actuarial evaluations.

Where insurance companies have an obligation to provide financial statements to proprietors or other users of financial statements, such statements may be prepared using statutory accounting practices or, more probably, in accordance with generally accepted accounting principles.

Generally Accepted Accounting Principles

The Cayman Islands' Insurance Law, 1979 requires that all licensed insurers prepare annual financial statements in accordance with generally accepted accounting principles (GAAP). Moreover, as part of the application procedure for an insurer's license, the company must indicate which GAAP will be adopted.

GAAP in the United States may be defined primarily in terms of the accounting standards issued by the American Institute of Certified Public Accountants (AICPA). In Canada, GAAP primarily consists of the accounting recommendations of the Canadian Institute of Chartered Accountants (CICA) and, in the United Kingdom, mainly by the Statements of Standard Accounting Practice issued by the Institute of Chartered Accountants in England and Wales (in association with other accountancy bodies in the United Kingdom).

However, because accounting for risk results in various peculiarities that are difficult to relate to certain basic concepts embodied in GAAP (such as matching revenue with expenses, i.e., premiums with claims), the following specific accounting guidelines exist dealing with property and casualty insurers:

- Statement of Financial Accounting Standards No. 60 (FASB 60) entitled "Accounting and Reporting by Insurance Enterprises" and issued June 1982 (which extracts specialized principles and practices from the AICPA insurance industry-related Guides and Statements of Position)

- CICA Accounting Guidelines on Financial Reporting by Property and Casualty Insurance Companies, issued April 1986.

- Compliance with GAAP would normally extend to the actual presentation of financial statements and footnote disclosure. The following is a summarized format of financial presentation for a captive engaged in general business, which would comply with GAAP and also be acceptable to the Cayman Islands' Superintendent of Insurance.

Balance Sheet

ASSETS	LIABLITIES AND SHAREHOLDERS EQUITY
	Liabilities
Bank balances	Accounts payable and accrued expenses
Marketable securities	Unearned premiums
Premiums receivable	Outstanding losses
Other receivables	
Other investments	
Total assets	Total liabilities
	Shareholders' equity
	Share capital
	Retained earnings
	Total shareholders' equity
	Total liabilities and shareholders' equity

Statement of Income and Retained Earnings

UNDERWRITING INCOME	UNDERWRITING EXPENSES
	Losses incurred
Premiums written	Losses paid
Premiums ceded	Increase in provision of outstanding losses
Change in unearned premiums	Other underwriting expenses
Net premiums earned	Total underwriting expenses
	Net underwriting income
General & administrative expenses	Net operating income
Income investment	Net income for the year
Retained earnings at beginning of year	Retained earnings at end of year

Premium Recognition and Loss Reserving

The two principal financial aspects of the underwriting cycle are the receipt of premiums, the major source of revenue to the insurer, and the payment of claims and establishment of reserves for payment of future claims, the prime obligations of the insurer. The method of recording premiums and the determination of adequate reserves to pay future losses represent the two most significant accounting policies for an insurer and the two most critical audit areas for the auditor.

The following is a summary of the recommendations of FASB 60 in relation to premiums and claims.

The recognition of premium income depends upon the duration of the insurance contract. Premiums from short-duration contracts are usually recognized as revenue over the period of the contract. The revenue is in proportion to the amount of insurance protection provided (i.e., evenly over the contract period). Premiums from long-duration contracts are recognized as revenue when due from policy holders.

A liability for unpaid claims relating to insurance contracts, including estimates of costs relating to incurred but not reported claims (IBNR), shall be accrued when insured events occur. This liability should be based on the estimated ultimate cost of settling the claims (including the effects of inflation and other social and economic factors), using past experience adjusted for current trends and any other factors that would modify past experience.

The typical offshore captive insurance company may experience particular difficulty in complying with these recommendations because:

Policies written by offshore captives are often subject to retrospective rating with a deposit premium subject to audit adjustment (such as audit of sales for product liability insurance or an audit of payrolls for workers' compensation insurance).

Some captives write policies that are, in substance, "funding policies," where the insurer actually assumes little or no risk and all or substantially all of the premiums are returnable to the insured by way of retrospective adjustment or policy dividend.

Captive reinsurers may receive incomplete premium and loss information from fronting companies, and may therefore have to adopt a reported basis of accounting and may experience considerable delays in receiving the reports.

The determination of loss reserves for captives can present difficulties if the business underwritten is of a specialist nature because of the lack of a record of historical loss experience or because it is too narrowly based to be statistically valid.

Many captives' historical loss experiences are inadequate for the purpose of performing a statistical evaluation and often prior historical loss experience records may not have been kept or may not be released by the previous insurer.

The Audit

Generally accepted auditing standards (GAAS), which relate to the auditors' qualifications, the performance of the examination, and reporting standards, also vary somewhat from country to country. However, international harmonization is gradually being achieved through the International Auditing Guidelines of the International Federation of

Accountants. It is not uncommon for the auditors' report on the financial statements of an offshore captive insurance company to be qualified on the basis of uncertainty with respect to premium recognition. Usually it is the inadequacy, or possibly an excess of reserves for outstanding losses due to the reasons stated above.

Glossary

A-B trust program: The commonly used grantor trust system used in the United States for estate planning.

arms-length transaction: A transaction between two related parties that is done in a way that is regular and bona fide.

asset diversification: The process of spreading the investment of your assets into a variety of different sectors or instruments.

"baby-boom" generation: The generation just after World War II that was noteworthy because of the large increase in babies born to parents during those years.

"baby-bust" generation: The generation that followed the baby boomers that was noteworthy because of the extreme swing in decrease **in babies born during those years.**

Bahamas: A former British colony off the shores of Florida that is know as an outstanding and reliable tax and business haven.

board of directors: Individuals elected or appointed by stockholders to direct the affairs of a company.

brass plate bank: Common name given to Class B banks in tax havens.

British Virgin Islands: An independent former British crown colony in the Caribbean that is now listed among the top business and tax havens of the world.

C-corporation: The common designation of a standard corporate structure in the United States.

captive insurance: Insurance that is created by and offered to a company or affinity group. It is generally not offered to the public.

Cayman Islands: A group of small islands south of Cuba that has grown into one of the major money centers of the world, the vast majority of which is legitimate international business transactions.

Channel Islands: A group of Islands off the coast of France that has been and continues to be a major off shore center for Europe. They include Jersey, Guernsey, and Sark.

charging order: A judges order that is allowed against the assets of a Limited Partnership. It allows for distributions to be paid to the judgment creditor but does not allow the dissolution of the partnership.

Class-A bank: A full service bank that is allowed to do business with the citizens in the jurisdiction where is licensed.

Class-B bank: A bank that is licensed to do business with non resident aliens of a certain jurisdiction. That is it can not do banking business with the residents of the jurisdiction that granted the license.

controlled foreign corporation (CFC): A foreign company where a United States citizen is deemed to be in control either by ownership of shares or control of the board of directors by virtue of proxy.

corporate ownership: Assets owned by a corporation.

corporation: A company limited by shares. The most common business structure in the world.

current account: The term applied to a regular checking account in most foreign banks.

direct mailing market: The marketing technique that uses mailing services to targeted lists of people whose names are compiled by market research and credit reporting firms.

domestic: Refers to business entities or people in your own jurisdiction. In a federation of states each of the states is domestic and the neighboring state is foreign. In the world community all of the United States, though each is an independent republic, is considered as domestic and the rest of the world is foreign.

dual-tracking: The process of setting up a number of companies to handle certain aspects of a business operation. This is useful in professional practices where certain aspects of the business can be contracted to a separate company set up for that reason.

European Common Market (ECM): To original concept of a unified Europe as outlined in the Treaty of Rome.

European Community (EC): The evolution of the ECM through the European Common Community (ECC) to the European Community (EC)

European Union (EU): The next stage in evolution. This was the name given to the community in the Mastrict Treaty that was ratified in 1993.

Family Limited Partnership (FLP): A limited partnership that is designed as a family estate planning tool. A majority of the limited partnership interest must be held by family members.

FIMBRA: Financial Intermediaries Managers & Brokers Regulatory Association. The British equivalent of our National Association of Securities Dealers NASD.

foreign: Refers to business entities or people in your own jurisdiction. In a federation of states each of the states is domestic and the neighboring state is foreign. In the world community all of the United States, though each is an independent republic, is considered as domestic and the rest of the world is foreign.

foreign banker: A banker in other jurisdictions outside the United States.

315

foreign-based corporation: A company limited by shares or limited by guarantee in a jurisdiction other than the one where you reside.

Fraudulent Conveyance Act: An act that is designed to protect creditors from the debtors ability to transfer assets out of reach. A judge can reverse the conveyance if it is deemed fraudulent.

General Partnership: A partnership between two or more individuals or companies. It can also be the controlling partner of a limited partnership.

Gibraltar: A tax haven off the coast of Spain that is often used by Europeans for tax planning because of its affiliation with the EC.

Grace Commission: A commission established by the government headed by Peter Grace that studied waste in government and made many recommendations for eliminating this waste, most of which was ignored by the bureaucracy.

gray-line: A term we give the idea of working in the gray area. Everything is not black and white, and there are tremendous savings to be made in the gray area of tax planning.

hard assets: Commonly considered to be Gold, Silver and other precious commodities.

hybrid captive: A captive insurance company that is created by a group of hybrid companies.

infrastructure: The underlying ability of a certain country to provide services to the companies that are established. For instance the number of accountants, tax lawyers, and bankers.

Intercon Associates, Ltd.: A company in Europe that offers company formation and management services to a large group of clients world wide. They are represented in the United States by LAD Financial Service and several other business and tax planning firms.

316

inter corporate billing: Billing for goods and services between companies. Must be at arms length.

international: Across national borders, synonymous with foreign in its applications.

international diversification: Spreading your assets into the international investment market.

investment committee: A group of people entrusted with the responsibility of investment of funds under its fiduciary control.

Iron Curtain: The countries that made up the former Soviet Union were considered to be behind the Iron Curtain.

Isle of Man: A small independent Island in the middle of the Irish Sea that is one of the most outstanding business and tax havens in the world.

junk bonds: High yield bonds that were made popular in the 80's through the process of corporate takeovers.

LAD Financial Services, Ltd.: A business consulting firm in Reno, Nevada that works with individuals and companies to design systems of domestic and international business and tax planning. They can be reached by calling 1-800-342-7553.

LaVera Tours, Inc.: The authors original foray into international business planning. A tour company that offered European continuing education tours to doctors.

Limited Partnership: A partnership where the limited partners are protected from liability while the general partner is responsible for the business operations.

living trust: The common trust created by an A-B trust system.

Malta: A Mediterranean business and tax haven.

Massachusetts business trust: A contractual company that is used for business purposes and treated as a trust for tax purposes. It is becoming a popular means of business operation that offers the business owner a certain degree of business privacy not offered by corporations.

Means Test: The test applied by the IRS when all else fails. They simply say if you have the means to acquire these assets you must have made this much money and apply the tax to that amount leaving you to prove your innocence.

multicorporate: Implies more than one corporation is involved in the business transaction or scheme.

offshore: Broadly defined, it is any jurisdiction outside of the one where you reside or under whose laws you are subject. More narrowly and commonly defined as those jurisdictions that are established as or have become the business or tax havens of the world. There are currently over 50 of them and many are Island Jurisdictions that were formerly part of the British Empire.

personal ownership: Owned by an individual.

personal service corporation: A company that is created by a professional that offers personal service to the public. Generally all of the stock in such a company must be held by the licensed individual.

Reagan Tax Reduction Act: One of many acts that were designed to reduce taxes. This particular reference is to the act of 1983, which dramatically reduced the tax rate and stimulated the economy to one of the longest and strongest growth cycles ever.

redlining: See gray-lining above.

Revenue Ruling 69-70: An IRS revenue ruling in 1969 that established the right of a foreign non-resident alien, individual or company, to create a trust and to name the United States resident or, citizen as a beneficiary. The money received by the US beneficiary is free of tax, which has lead to some creative abuse by certain non-professional tax planners.

RICO: Racketeer, Influence, & Corrupt Organization act o 1984. A broad federal act under which many crimes are included.

risk model: A model created by demographics that determines the risk that a certain group or individual will have under the plan.

S-corporation: Formerly called a "Sub-Chapter S" corporation. This is a corporate structure created in the United States that is recognized as a company for business purposes but treated as a partnership for tax purposes. It is tax transparent and passes its profit or loss through to its owners. It is becoming obsolete with the creation and tax approval of the Limited Liability Company.

shares: Tokens of ownership in a company usually shown as stock certificates.

small business corporation: A closely held company that operates a business. Usually all the shares are held by less than 35 members.

stocks: Synonymous with shares.

tax transparent: A business entity that is not subject to tax on its own right. The possible tax exposure is passed through to the owner of the entity, such as the members of the partnership, or members of the Limited Liability Company or the stockholders of the S-Corporation.

Tetra Test: A term we give the five most important tests that the IRS uses to determine tax liability for foreign involvement by United States citizens.

triple A-rated bank: The highest rating that the international community gives to banks. There are few of them in the world and at this time The United States has none.

trust: A contract that establishes the rights of the grantor, the trustee, and the beneficiary in an estate planning model. Trusts are also used for tax planning and for business planning.

umbrella mutual funds: Mutual funds that do not distribute earnings to the shareholders but instead roll up the profits within the fund and show it as increased value. These funds also are commonly held in fund families that allow transfer of interest between funds which make it possible to roll up profits without the need to declare them or to recognize them for tax purposes.

underwriting committee: A committee of an insurance company that determines the rate of insurance a certain policy holder or class of policy holders will pay.

Uniform Fraudulent Transfer Act: An act that is designed to bring under one definition the possible acts of fraudulent transfer of the various States. Uniform laws are a requirement of federal legal planning when it is clearly recognized in the constitution that we are a federation of individual and independent states.

upstream: The process of paying invoices to a company in a low tax state by a company in a high tax state. This makes it possible to move potentially taxable profit to the company in the state with the lowest tax exposure.

world-class bank: Generally considered to be the AA and AAA rated banks of the world.

Acknowledgments

So much to say and so little space...I would like to gratefully acknowledge the following people.

First, Berny Dohrmann, President of Income Builders International, whose inspiration at the June 1993 Free Enterprise Forum in Long Beach served to focus my attention on the need to get this project going. When he says "Do The Dream!" you realize that nothing holds you back except your own inertia. Thanks Berny, here is my WOW!

A special thanks to my many friends and colleagues in the International Tax Planning Association, especially Marshall Langer, Denis Kleinfeld, and Milton Grundy whose quick answers to my many questions made my learning about this business such a pleasure.

To my friend and colleague, John Fitzgerald in Cork, Ireland, who as administrator of so many companies for us and many other international advisors, offers such clear and concise thinking in his friendly Irish manner that draws you in. Thanks John, I could not do it without you.

I would like to acknowledge and remember the invaluable resource of the late Peter Redmond at the Offshore Institute, where I am a charter member, and note that I have in my library the complete set of the institute journal and have turned many times to that resource material. I miss Peter and the chats we would have on each of my trips to The Isle of Man. He was such a help and gave of his time so freely, our industry has lost a giant.

My heartfelt thanks also to Reg Newton, Charles Cain and Peter Bond, who in the early stages of my education and training offered so much. And to Barry Spitz who I see as one of the great strategic planners in the offshore world. His "Tom and Jerry" stories have great impact and his creative solutions are a joy to study. The ideas and thoughts of these individuals are sprinkled throughout this book and I will be forever grateful to you.

Finally, to those early clients who, with encouragement and assistance, urged me to put my original lecture notes into book form. This resulted in the first version of this book, "Off Shore Options for Small Businesses". Without that gentle push, this project might never have been started.

My sincere thanks to Catherine E. Haynes, my editor, "word merchant," and consultant, whose expert polishing of these rough drafts, whose patient understanding of the whims and desires of this writer, and whose expertise in the field of publishing was directly instrumental in the success of this final edition.

I am forever grateful...

Dr. Larry Turpen

INDEX

About the Author

Larry Turpen, DDS, practiced dentistry for 25 years from 1962–1987. He sold his practice to devote full time to his second source of income, international tax and business service. Dr. Turpen is president and CEO of LAD Financial Services of Reno, Nevada, and Managing Director of Intercon Associates, Ltd., an international business planning organization. Since 1986, Dr. Turpen has given presentations at business seminars and symposiums around the world. He is the author of the following three books.

> *Offshore Options for Small Businesses*
> *Creative Strategies for Privacy, Protection and Profit*
> *How and Why Americans Go Offshore*

These books were written in response to many requests for detailed information on foreign–based corporations.

Additional Information

Intercon Associates

Established in 1983, Intercon Associates is an Isle of Man company that assists U.S. citizens in establishing and managing their foreign business entities.

If you are interested in obtaining more information regarding:

1. A private consultation to answer all your questions with regard to out of state corporate jurisdictions.

2. Advice on the best business structure to meet your objective.

3. How to form a Nevada Corporation or Limited Liability Company within 10 days.

4. How to become a qualified consultant in your area.

5. Obtaining a business plan.

6. To order additional copies this book.
   (Allow 2-4 weeks for UPS delivery)

Contact LAD Financial Services by mail, phone or FAX.

LAD Financial Services
1005 Terminal Way #110
Reno, Nevada 89502

Telephone: (702) 324-0211   1
FAX: (702) 324-6266